CLASSIC

BRAIN TWISTERS

CLASSIC

BRAIN TWISTERS

By Derrick Niederman,
Jaime & Lea Poniachik,
Tim Sole, and Rod Marshall

Main Street
A division of Sterling Publishing Co., Inc.
New York

10 9 8 7 6 5 4 3 2 1

Published by Sterling Publishing Co., Inc.
387 Park Avenue South, New York, NY 10016
© 2005 by Sterling Publishing Co., Inc.

Material in this collection was adapted from
Sit & Solve Brainteasers, © 2003 by Derrick Niederman
Hard-to-Solve Brainteasers, © 1978 and 1996 by Jaime and Lea Poniachik
You'd Better Be Really Smart Brain Bafflers, © 2003 by Tim Sole and Rod Marshall

Distributed in Canada by Sterling Publishing
℅ Canadian Manda Group, 165 Dufferin Street
Toronto, Ontario, Canada M6K 3H6
Distributed in Great Britain by Chrysalis Books Group PLC
The Chrysalis Building, Bramley Road, London W10 6SP, England
Distributed in Australia by Capricorn Link (Australia) Pty. Ltd.
P.O. Box 704, Windsor, NSW 2756, Australia

Sterling ISBN 1-4027-2360-1

CLASSIC
BRAIN
TWISTERS

CONTENTS

INTRODUCTION

These brainteasers have two purposes: to let you have fun and to train your mind. You don't need any special knowledge to solve them. It's a matter of thinking a little about the questions and applying common sense.

The puzzles are organized by order of complexity, from quick teasers to twisters, and up to bafflers, but all should be fun to solve. If you get stumped, the answers are in the back of the book, broken down by section. Once you learn the logic behind an answer, it may help you solve some other problems. The middle section, Tough Twisters, has some hints at the end of the section for additional help.

Solving brainteasers can be a good activity for a solo player or a group and can be turned into a game of competition.

MIND TEASERS

THE HARD WAY

In this word ladder, your task is to convert the word PASSER into the word SPARSE, by switching two adjacent letters at a time, in five moves. Write each interim step on one of the blank lines.

P A S S E R

_____

_____

_____

_____

S P A R S E

Answer, page 198

WHO'S NEXT?

What is the next number in the following sequence?

(There are two possible answers.)

17, 19, 23, 29, ?

Answer, page 198

CODE DEPENDENCE

Using the standard alphanumeric code of A = 1, B = 2, and so on, what word is represented by the sequence 3 1 2 1 2 5?

Answer, page 198

WET AND WILD

A cat watched a bird fly back and forth. Finally, the cat could take it no more. Seeing its chance, the cat jumped…and caught the bird in mid-flight. Nearby rescuers arrived only seconds later. Although the cat had no time to harm the bird, it was not alive. What had happened?

Answer, page 198

TWO FOR ONE

For each pair of words or expressions below, there is a single word definition (or crossword clue) for both of them. Can you find the definitions?

MOROSE	**GROSS**	**HOT DOG**	**BALL**
INDIGO	**MAJOR**	**CANDID**	**BEEF**

Answer, page 199

TAKING NOTES

The diagram below describes what common three-word expression?

Answer, page 199

BRICK BY BRICK

The diagram below shows one face of a chimney. No bricks were cut to form the chimney; the "half-bricks" are the ends of bricks that extend along one of the other sides. How many bricks were needed to build the entire chimney?

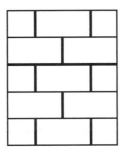

Answer, page 199

ENDLESS SUMMER

Suppose that the song "99 Bottles of Beer on the Wall" was sung from beginning to end. What would be the sum of all the numbers (including repeats) in the song?

Answer, page 200

FIVE OF A KIND

A. A puzzle book once challenged its readers to form an expression using five 3's so that the result would be 37. No problem: 33 + 3 + 3/3 does the trick. But can you find another way?

B. Similarly 44 + 44/4 = 55. But can you form 55 using five 4's in a completely different way?

Answer, page 200

HALF A SHAKE

If two earthquakes are a point apart on the Richter scale, then the one with the higher reading is ten times as powerful as the other. Suppose the two earthquakes differ by half a point. How much more powerful is the one with the higher reading?

Answer, page 200

IN THE MIDDLE

What words contain the following letter sequences? (There may be multiple solutions. How many can you find?)

ILLILI   **HTH**   **IQUA**   **AWB**

Answer, page 200

SURE THING

A woman wants to surprise her husband with a new ride-on mower for Christmas, which is still several days away. Unfortunately, the only place to put the new mower is in a tool shed. It is secured by a combination lock, but her husband of course knows the combination. Nonetheless, she has the store deliver the mower to the shed, and on Christmas morning has her husband open the lock, certain that he wasn't aware that a new mower was inside. How could she be so sure?

Answer, page 200

CLOSE QUARTERS

Place a quarter on a table or flat surface. Place another quarter to the right, just touching the first one. Keep going around in a circle, with each new quarter touching the center one and the one just placed. By the time you complete the circle, how many quarters will you have placed around the middle one?

Answer, page 201

BASE TEN

Suppose the numerical pyramid below kept on going. What would be the sum of the numbers in the 10th row?

Answer, page 201

SEEING STARS

Each of the actors or actresses in the left-hand column can be paired with one of the musical groups or single artists in the right-hand column. Can you find the rule that brings these performers together?

Diahann Carroll	**Harry Chapin**
Alex Trebek	**The Beatles**
Jimmy Walker	**The Rolling Stones**
Danny DeVito	**The Greg Kihn Band**
Donna Pescow	**Chic**

Answer, page 201

FENDER BENDER

Two cars traveling on Warren Street had each just passed Redington Road when they had an accident. Remarkably, both cars sustained damage to their *front* fenders. How is this possible?

Answer, page 202

DOUBLE CROSS–I

Create two independent solutions to the following mini-crossword:

ACROSS

1. Colorado, Missouri, or Mississippi

3. Tooth _____

DOWN

1. Inflexible

2. Anagram of "layer"

Solution 1

1			2
3			

Solution 2

1			2
3			

Answer, page 202

ICE FOLLIES

Suppose a women's figure skating competition is held among five skaters. A skater's score equals her placement (1 through 5) in the short program multiplied by ½, plus her placement in the long program. For example, if a skater finishes fourth in the short program and third in the long program, her total score would be $4(\frac{1}{2}) + 3 = 5$. In case of a tie, the skater who did better in the long program wins.

Let's suppose, now, that the order for the short program was A, B, C, D, and E. It turns out that after the long program, there was a three-way tie for first place. Who won?

Answer, page 202

HIDDEN PATTERN

What do the following four seven-letter words have in common?

REALIGN   **SHALLOT**
CHARRED   **INDULGE**

Answer, page 203

SIGN OF THE TIMES

There are infinitely many pairs of numbers whose sum equals their product. But there is one only solution to the pair of equations below, assuming that A, B, C, D, and E each stand for a single, distinct digit.

$AB \times C.DE = AB + C.DE$

Can you find the solution?

Answer, page 203

ODD MAN OUT

The following four men all have the three letters LEN somewhere in their names. Which one does not belong?

JAY LENO
VLADIMIR LENIN
LEN DEIGHTON
STEVE ALLEN

Answer, page 203

CHECKERBOARD SQUARE

Below is a 2 by 2 checkerboard in which four gray oversized checkers have been placed: The diameter of each checker is equal to the length of a square.

How many such checkers fit inside a standard 8 by 8 board?

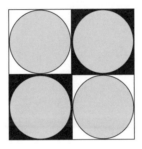

Answer, page 203

TIME WARP

Under what circumstances could the time in a state bordering the Atlantic be the same as the time in a state bordering the Pacific?

Answer, page 204

SPEED DIALING

One morning a housewife calls her husband from their home and asks him if he wants to go out to dinner that evening. He says "Yes," so she says she'll call the restaurant to confirm a time. They hang up, and she calls the restaurant to make sure that 7:30 is okay. When she calls her husband back, she uses the redial button, even though she had called the restaurant in between. How is this possible?

(Assume that both the husband and the restaurant had caller ID, and that the same number showed up—meaning that no cell phone or second line was involved.)

Answer, page 204

A PERFECT STRANGER

A woman went into town carrying an object in her right hand. Before she had reached her destination, a man came up to her and asked, "Can I take that?" She said, "Please do," even though the man was a total stranger. What did the woman have in her hand?

Answer, page 204

A SECOND KIND OF CUT

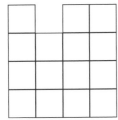

The diagram at left is a 4 by 4 grid with a square cut out. The shape can be separated into two pieces of the same shape (though of different sizes), as shown below.

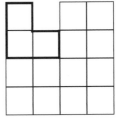

Can you think of an entirely different way of dividing the shape into two pieces of the same shape? (The divisions do not all have to be along the grid lines.)

Answer, page 204

ATTENTION SPORTS FANS

What number belongs in the slot with the question mark?

1	2	3	4	5	6	7	8	9	10
0	1	1	1	1	3	2	4	4	?

Answer, page 205

SHOW TIME

Place a letter in each of the seven boxes below to form three three-letter classic TV shows:

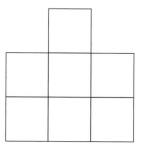

Answer, page 205

STAYING THE SAME

No one could argue with the following equation:

$$\sqrt{10} - 3 = \sqrt{10} - 3$$

But can you add three lines to the right side of the equation so that the equation still holds true?

Answer, page 206

WORD CHAIN

Insert words into the blanks to create a chain of two-word expressions or compound words beginning with KEY and ending with HORSE, then the other way around:

KEY

— — — — —

— — — — — —

— — — — — — —

— — — —

— — —

HORSE

HORSE

— — —

— — — —

— — — — —

— — — — —

— — — — —

— — —

KEY

Answer, page 206

HAPPY ANNIVERSARY

A summer camp was started in 1965. The owner staged a big celebration for his 35th season running the camp. In which century did that celebration take place—the 20th or the 21st?

Answer, page 206

SHORT BUT SWEET

What is the smallest number of pitches that a pitcher can pitch and still come away with a complete game? (A *real* complete game; nothing rain-shortened or anything like that.)

Answer, page 206

PICKING UP STICKS

A. Suppose you had five sticks of lengths 1, 2, 3, 4, and 5 inches. If you chose three of them at random, what is the likelihood that the three sticks could be put together, tip to tip, so as to form a triangle?

B. Now suppose you had twenty sticks, of lengths 1 through 20 inches. If you picked three at random, what is the likelihood that the three could be put together, tip to tip, so as to form a right triangle?

Answer, page 207

ALL WET

A couple went for a drive with the sunroof wide open. They kept the sunroof open even though a thunderstorm erupted, and they didn't get wet.

Another driver happened to see that peculiar sight and opened his sunroof—only to get soaking wet a short while later. Care to explain?

Answer, page 207

SPACE SAVERS

What do the eight following three-letter words have in common?

fat	oak	lax	sat
den	sea	pit	lit

Answer, page 207

ROMAN CROSSWORD

This crossword has no numbers for the clues, but plenty of numbers in the entries themselves. Every entry is either a word or a number in Roman numeral form.

The clues are in no particular order:
The trick is to figure out where everything goes!

ACROSS

WORDS	NUMBERS
Really angry	151
Type of pride	1910
Poorly lit	4
Doogie	21
Howser, ___	69
Type of	905
audio file	2003
	1155
	60
	2
	1901
	3000
	160
	156

DOWN

WORDS	NUMBERS
Fort ___	3
Actress	56
Kennedy	1600
Mingle	2009
"Courteous"	52
war?	150
Morrow	2015
Pickle type	706
	2200
	1011
	2060
	6
	1110

Answer, page 208

THE MAX FACTOR

When the bleachers at a high school basketball game were filled to capacity, they held 319 people. Assuming that each row contained the same number of people, how many rows were there?

Answer, page 208

ON THE LINE

A basketball player who makes 80 percent of his free throws goes to the foul line near the end of a very close game: His team trails by two with just 1.7 seconds remaining. If he makes both of his foul shots, the game will go into overtime.

What is the probability that he will make only one of two?

Answer, page 208

BINARY OPERATION

What is the smallest number consisting of only 0's and 1's that is divisible by 15?

Answer, page 209

QUIT WHILE YOU'RE AHEAD

Two men are playing Russian roulette using a pistol with six chambers. Assuming that a single bullet is used and that the cylinder is spun after every turn, what is the probability that the first man will lose the game?

Answer, page 209

GETTING SHEEPISH

This one's been around but hasn't gotten the attention it deserves. We start with a one-acre tract of land shaped like a right triangle. At the midpoint of the hypotenuse is a post, to which a dog is tethered with a rope just long enough to reach the endpoints of the hypotenuse. There are also posts at each of the midpoints of the other two legs of the triangle; each has a post, and to each post is tethered a sheep. Again, the ropes are just long enough to permit both sheep to reach the endpoints of their respective legs.

The question is this: In how much space outside the original tract of land can the sheep graze without having to worry about the dog reaching them?

Answer, page 209

DOUBLE CROSS–II

If you liked the first Double Cross, here's your second chance. Create two independent solutions to the following mini-crossword:

ACROSS
1. Caesar, for one
3. Grout and mortar guy

DOWN
1. ____ whale
2. Anagram of "dinar"

Solution 1

1			2
3			

Solution 2

1			2
3			

Answer, page 210

CIRCULAR REASONING

If three points are placed at random around the circumference of a circle, what is the probability that all three will reside in some semicircle, as in the diagram below?

Answer, page 210

NORSE CODE

What four-letter man's name has the same property as each of the two and three-letter combinations below?

ga   sli   smo   wi   bo   la   fea

Answer, page 211

BACK AND FORTH

Take a two-digit number. Square it. Reverse the three (distinct) digits of its square. Take the square root. Reverse the two digits of that number, and you have the original two-digit number. What is that number?

Answer, page 211

BUMPER CROP

A farmer tells his son to select five watermelons to bring to town to be sold at the weekly farmer's market. Because the watermelons are sold by weight, they must be put on a scale before the trip into town, but the son makes a teensy-weensy mistake. Instead of weighing them individually, he weighs them in pairs. These are the weights he comes up with, in pounds:

20, 22, 23, 24, 25, 26, 27, 28, 30, 31

How much does each of the watermelons weigh?

Answer, page 211

TWO GUYS

You may never have noticed, but the word "melted" consists of two mens' first names placed back-to-back. Now it's your turn. Put together two men's names to form:

1) a fish
2) a flower
3) a type of shampoo
4) a carom
5) a Canadian province

Answer, page 212

SQUARE DEAL

Imagine a 24 by 24 chessboard. Suppose you started counting all of the "sub-squares" of the chessboard: squares of lengths 1 through 24 found by tracing the sides of the squares of the big board. To remind you how many sub-squares you've counted, you make a pile of little squares (which you just happen to have around), one little square for each sub-square. It turns out that these little squares can be put together to form an even bigger square chessboard. What is the length of each side of this gigantic board?

Answer, page 212

DON'T FEEL STUMPED

The diagram below shows an evergreen tree. As it happens, the shape of the tree makes it possible to draw a circle around the tree as shown. How tall is the stump of the tree in relation to the entire tree?

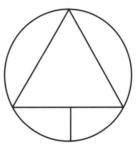

Answer, page 212

NOT-SO-TRUE CRIME

The murder weapon was a rifle, but the victim was not shot. The cause of death was asphyxiation. A clever plot, but can you bring the perpetrator to justice? What in the world happened?

Answer, page 213

OUT OF SIGHT

The name of Candice Bergen contains the hidden word "iceberg." Can you find the celebrities whose names contain the following hidden words?

NONE

MARSH

LIEN

Answer, page 213

THE DATING GAME

The date July 14, 1998 has the property that when written out in numeric form—i.e., 7/14/98—the year equals the product of the day and month. During the 1950s, which years had no dates with this property?

Answer, page 213

WHAT'S IN A NAME?

The actress Lee Grant has a name consisting of two Civil War generals. What actor or actress has a name consisting of:

1) two presidents?
2) two New York City mayors?
3) two cowboy portrayers?

Answer, page 213

ROADS SCHOLARSHIP

Finish this story by filling in each blank with the name of a U.S. college or university.

A reckless driver had caused an accident on a _____ highway. Unfortunately for him, he was booked by the nastiest _____ police history. The driver tried to make excuses: "With all that fog, I couldn't _____ thing out there, and the rain made me _____ ." At that point, the man in blue responded angrily, "Look, mister, either you make _____ spend the night in jail."

Answer, page 213

MORE FUN WITH DATES

A set of three whole numbers {A, B, C} that satisfies the equation $A^2 + B^2 = C^2$ is called a Pythagorean triple. (The Pythagorean Theorem states that the three legs of any right triangle must satisfy that equation.)

What will be the last date in the 21st century that, when written out in Month/Day/Year notation, forms a Pythagorean triple? Note that March 4th, 2005 (3/04/05) is one such date, because $3^2 + 4^2 = 5^2$. However, it is not the last date in the century to fit the bill. Can you find that date?

Answer, page 214

OPEN AND SHUT CASE

A man lived by himself in a house with a very small bathroom. Things were so crowded in the bathroom that one of the drawers to the vanity wouldn't open all the way unless you put in some extra effort. However, every couple of weeks or so, the drawer could be pulled out quite easily. What was the problem?

Answer, page 214

THE BLACK HOLE

The pieces in the upper left diagram have been rearranged and placed in the lower right diagram. What happened to the hole?

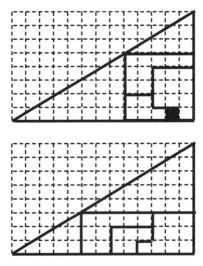

Answer, page 214

SWEET SIXTEEN

Arrange the numbers from 1 through 16 in a 4 by 4 square such that the sum of each of the four columns is the same. (There is more than one solution.)

Answer, page 215

NO RULER NEEDED

Below are three quarter-circles, each of which is divided into two equal areas by a straight line. Which line is the longest? The shortest?

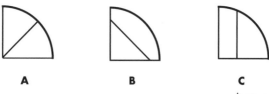

A   B   C

Answer, page 215

TOUGH NEIGHBORHOOD

Place the digits 1 through 8 in the boxes below so that no two consecutive numbers are in bordering boxes.

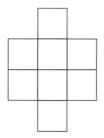

Answer, page 215

WHAT NOW?

Consider the listing of ten words given below:

Gown
Jab
Trajectory
Jam
Jump
Jacquard
Ajar
Movable
Which
Jet

Which word comes next?

1) Javelin   2) Muffin   3) Jackpot   4) Ziti

Answer, page 216

CUTTING CORNERS

The rectangle in the corner is twice as long as it is wide. How many of these rectangles will fit in the square?

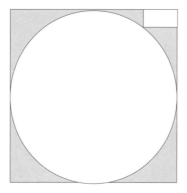

Answer, page 216

TOUGH TWISTERS

TWINS

Peter and Paul are twin brothers. One of them (we don't know which) always lies. The other one always tells the truth. I ask one of them:

"Is Paul the one that lies?"

"Yes," he answers.

Did I speak to Peter or Paul?

Hint, page 107 / Answer, page 218

TWIN STATISTICS

Suppose that 3% of births give rise to twins. What percentage of the population is a twin: 3%, less than 3%, or more than 3%?

Hint, page 107 / Answer, page 218

PLACE YOUR CARDS

You have three cards: an ace, a queen, and a six. One is a diamond, one is a heart, and one is a spade, although not necessarily in that order.

The diamond sits between the queen and the heart.

The six is immediately to the right of the spade.
Write in the picture below where each card is located.

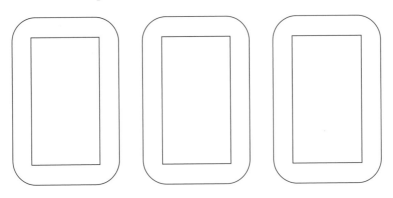

Hint, page 107 / Answer, page 218

THE PROFESSOR AND HIS FRIEND

Professor Zizoloziz puts 40 matches on the table and explains a game to his friend Kathy.

Each player in turn takes 1, 3, or 5 matches. The winner is the one who takes the last match. Kathy chooses to go first and takes 3 matches.

Who do you think will win this game, Kathy or the professor?

Hint, page 107 / Answer, page 218

IRREGULAR CIRCUIT

✦✦✦

Two cars start from point A at the same time and drive around a circuit more than one mile in length. While they are driving laps around the circuit, each car must maintain a steady speed. Since one car is faster than the other, one car will pass the other at certain points. The first pass occurs 150 yards from point A.

At what distance from A will one car pass the other again?

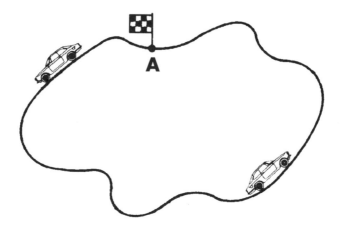

Hint, page 107 / Answer, page 218

ECONOMICAL PROGRESSION

Below are four terms in an arithmetic progression (a series in which the difference between terms is constant, in this case 50):

5, 55, 105, 155

Notice how the four terms use only three different digits: 0, 1, and 5.

Can you find six terms in an arithmetic progression that use only three different digits?

Hint, page 107 / Answer, page 218

SKIN AND SHOES

A white man is wearing a pair of white shoes, a black man is wearing a pair of black shoes, and a red-skinned man is wearing a pair of red shoes. In a gesture of friendship, they decide to exchange shoes. When they are done, each man has on one shoe from each of the other two men.

How many shoes will you have to look at to know which color of shoe each man is wearing on each foot; that is, which color shoe each man wears on his right foot and which color each man wears on his left foot? Note that when you look at a shoe, you can see that man's skin color.

Hint, page 107 / Answer, page 219

EVE'S ENIGMA

After heaven, the earth, the grass, and all the animals were created, the snake, who was very smart, decided to make its own contribution.

It decided to lie every Tuesday, Thursday and Saturday. For the other days of the week, it told the truth.

"Eve, dear Eve, why don't you try an apple?" the snake suggested.

"But I am not allowed to!" said Eve.

"Oh, no!" said the snake. "You can eat it today since it is Saturday and God is resting."

"No, not today," said Eve, "Maybe tomorrow."

"Tomorrow is Wednesday and it will be too late," insisted the snake.

This is how the snake tricked Eve.

What day of the week did this conversation take place?

Hint, page 108 / Answer, page 219

WHAT MONTH—I

A month begins on a Friday and ends on a Friday, too. What month is it?

Hint, page 108 / Answer, page 219

WHAT MONTH—II

The result of adding the date of the last Monday of last month and the date of the first Thursday of next month is 38. If both dates are of the same year, what is the current month?

Hint, page 108 / Answer, page 219

UP AND DOWN

This morning I had to take the stairs because the elevator was out of service. I had already gone down seven steps when I saw Professor Zizoloziz on the ground floor coming up. I continued descending at my usual pace, greeted the professor when we passed, and was surprised to see that when I still had four more steps to go, the professor had gone up the whole flight. "When I go down one step, he goes up two," I thought.

How many steps does the staircase have?

Hint, page 108 / Answer, page 219

BROKEN M

We have formed six triangles by drawing three straight lines on the M. That's not enough. Starting with a new M, form nine triangles by drawing three straight lines.

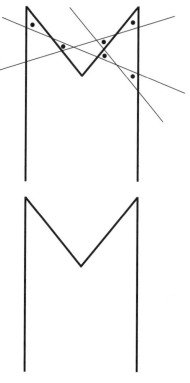

Hint, page 108 / Answer, page 220

SOCCER SCORES—I

A soccer tournament has just ended. Five teams participated and each one played once against each of the other teams. The winner of a match received 2 points, the losing team 0 points, and each team received 1 point for a tie.

The final results were:

Lions	6 points
Tigers	5 points
Bears	3 points
Orioles	1 point

We are missing one team, the Eagles. What was their point total?

Hint, page 108 / Answer, page 220

SOCCER SCORES—II

In a three-team tournament, each team played once against each of the two other teams. Each team scored one goal.

The final results were:

Lions	3 points
Tigers	2 points
Bears	1 point

What was the score in each match?

Hint, page 108 / Answer, page 220

PROHIBITED CONNECTION

Using numbers 1, 2, 3, 4, 5, and 6, put each of them in a circle. There is only one condition. The circles connected by a line cannot have consecutive numbers. For example, 4 cannot be connected with 3 or 5.

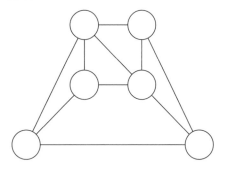

Hint, page 108 / Answer, page 220

WHAT TIME IS IT—I

I'm looking at my watch. From this moment on, the hour hand will take exactly twice as long as the minute hand to reach the number six. What time is it?

Hint, page 108 / Answer, page 221

WHAT TIME IS IT—II

I'm looking at my watch. From this moment on, the hour hand will take exactly three times longer than the minute hand to reach the number six. What time is it?

Hint, page 108 / Answer, page 221

WHAT TIME IS IT—III

I'm looking at my watch. The hour hand is on one mark and the minute hand is on the next one. (By marks, we mean minute marks.) What time is it?

Hint, page 108 / Answer, page 221

WHAT TIME IS IT—IV

I'm looking at my watch. The hour hand is on one mark and the minute hand is on the previous one. (By marks, we mean minute marks.) What time is it?

Hint, page 108 / Answer, page 221

CONCENTRIC

The big square has an area of 60 square inches. Is there a fast way to figure out what the area of the small square is?

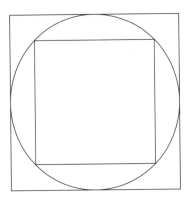

Hint, page 109 / Answer, page 222

JOHN CASH

John Cash saw his face on a poster nailed to a tree. As he approached, he saw "WANTED, DEAD OR ALIVE." Under his picture, it read "REWARD: ___ DOLLARS."

There was a three-digit figure on the poster. John drew his Colt and shot at the first number (in the hundreds column).

He had just reduced the price on his head by five times.

"Good Lord!" said the doctor's daughter, who was sitting on the other side of the tree doing her math homework.

John blushed, and shot again at another number (in the tens column).

He had just reduced the price on his head by another five times.

"Nice shooting!" said the young girl.

"Thank you, miss," said John. He spurred his horse and never returned.

What was the initial reward offered on John's head?

Hint, page 109 / Answer, page 222

NEW RACE

Two cars start traveling from two different points and in opposite directions in a circuit race at a constant speed. The cars cross for the first time at point A. The second time is at point B. The third time is at point C, and the fourth one is again at point A.

How much faster is one car going than the other?

Hint, page 109 / Answer, page 222

RUSSIAN ROULETTE

Russian roulette was created by Count Ugo Lombardo Fiumiccino, who successfully died during his first presentation of it.

He placed six jars on a shelf, as in the drawing below. After staring at them, he closed his eyes and told his friend to fill them up with the ingredients, making sure that each jar contained an ingredient other than the one shown on its label.

When she was finished, the count asked:

"Dear Petrushka, would you be so kind as to tell me where the salt is?"

"Under the jar containing snuff," answered Petrushka.

"My dear friend, would you tell me where the sugar is?" he asked.

"Immediately to the right of the jar containing coffee," she answered.

Ugo Lombardo Fiumiccino, confirming his desire to commit suicide, reached immediately for the jar containing arsenic.

Where is the arsenic?

Hint, page 109 / Answer, page 223

THE CALCULATOR KEYS

Several times Professor Zizoloziz mentioned that he feels uncomfortable looking at his pocket calculator. Yesterday, he was elated because he had found the reason why. The layout of the keys from 1 to 9 and the "minus" and "equal" signs look like they are doing subtraction. It's an incorrect one however, because 789 minus 456 does not equal 123. Zizoloziz thought of changing the numbers to achieve a correct equation. He changed 7 with 3, then 3 with 4, and 9 with 6, resulting in 486 − 359 = 127. He made only three changes to achieve this.

Using the keypad below as a reference, can you obtain a correctly subtracted number with only two changes?

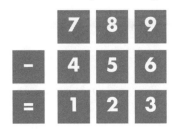

Hint, page 109 / Answer, page 223

NICE DISCOUNTS

A bookstore has a nice discount policy. If you buy a $20 book today, you get a 2% discount on your next purchase. If you buy a $15 book, you get a 1.5% discount on your next purchase. If you have to buy three books that cost $10, $20, and $30, you could buy the $30 book today, the $10 tomorrow (on which you'll get a 3% discount), and the $20 book the following day (on which you'll get a 1% discount). Or you could buy the $30 book and the $20 book today, and the $10 book tomorrow (with a 5% discount).

What is the cheapest way to buy five books priced at $10, $20, $30, $40, and $50?

Hint, page 109 / Answer, page 223

HOROSCOPE

An indiscreet young man asks his beautiful mathematics teacher her age. She responds, "Today's date is my age, although before this week is over there will be another day with a date one fifth of the new age that I will be."

What is the teacher's sign of the zodiac?

Hint, page 109 / Answer, page 223

ENIGMATIC FARES

Professor Zizoloziz always adds the five digits on a bus transfer. Yesterday, he rode route 62 with a friend. As soon as he got the tickets, which were consecutively numbered, he added the numbers on them and then told his friend that the sum of all ten digits was exactly 62. His logical friend asked him if the sum of the numbers on either of the tickets was by any chance 35. Professor Zizoloziz answered and his friend then knew the numbers on the bus tickets.

What were the numbers on the two bus tickets?

Hint, page 109 / Answer, page 224

MONTE CARLO

The famous playboy Hystrix Tardigradus explained to a beautiful woman his system for playing roulette:

"In each round, I always bet half of the money I have at the time on red. Yesterday, I counted and I had won as many rounds as I had lost."

Over the course of the night, did Hystrix win, lose, or break even?

Hint, page 109 / Answer, page 224

STRANGERS IN THE NIGHT

The midnight train is coming down the Strujen-Bajen Mountains. Art Farnanski seems to be dozing off in his seat.

Someone knows that this is not true.

At the station, all the passengers get off the train, except one. The conductor comes and taps him on the shoulder to let him know they have arrived. Art Farnanski does not answer. He is dead.

"His heart?" asks commander Abrojos, looking at the dead body.

"Strychnine," answers the forensic doctor.

Hours later, the four people that had shared the train compartment with the dead man are at the police station.

The man in the dark suit:
"I'm innocent. The blonde woman was talking to Farnanski."

The blonde woman:
"I'm innocent. I did not speak to Farnanski."

The man in the light suit:
"I'm innocent. The brunette woman killed him."

The brunette woman:
"I'm innocent. One of the men killed him."

That same morning, while he is serving him coffee, the waiter at the Petit Piccolo asks commander Abrojos:

"This is an easy case for you, isn't it?"

"Yes," answers the commander. "Four true statements and four false ones. Easy as pie."

Who killed Farnanski? (Only one person is guilty.)

Hint, page 109 / Answer, page 224

THE FOREIGNERS AND THE MENU

A particular inn always offers the same nine dishes on its dinner menu: A, B, C, D, E, F, G, H, and I.

Five foreigners arrive. Nobody tells them which dish corresponds to each letter and so they each select one letter without knowing what they will eat.

The innkeeper arrives with the five dishes ordered and puts them in the center of the table so that they can decide who eats what.

This goes on for two more nights.

The foreigners, who are professors of logic, were able to deduce by the dishes they ordered which letter represents what dish.

What could have been the dishes ordered each of the three nights?

Hint, page 110 / Answer, page 225

FORT KNOX JUMPING FROGS—I

The first puzzle of this series is very well known. We included it here, though, because it is good practice for the following puzzles, since they all use the same method of moving coins.

Make a line of eight coins. In four moves, make four piles of two coins each.

A move consists of taking one coin, skipping over two others, and piling it on top of the next one.

The answers list one of several possible solutions for all of the puzzles in this series.

Hint, page 110 / Answer, page 225

FORT KNOX JUMPING FROGS—II

Place 14 coins in the shape of a cross, as shown in the illustration. In seven moves as described in the puzzle on page 62, make seven piles of two coins each. Note: Only move the coins in a straight line; do not change directions.

Hint, page 110 / Answer, page 225

FORT KNOX JUMPING FROGS—III

Place 12 coins on the three rings as shown in the illustration below. In six moves as described in the puzzle on page 62, make six piles of two coins each. Note: Only move the coins around their own rings and always go clockwise in direction.

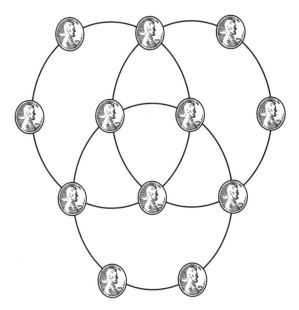

Hint, page 110 / Answer, page 226

FORT KNOX JUMPING FROGS—IV

Place 20 coins in the shape of a star as shown in the illustration below. In ten moves as described in the puzzle on page 62, make ten piles of two coins each. Note: Only move the coins along the straight lines and do not turn corners.

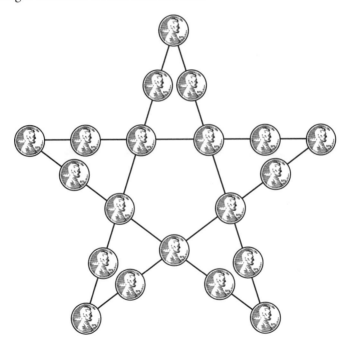

Hint, page 110 / Answer, page 226

FORT KNOX JUMPING FROGS—V

Place 20 coins in a four-by-five rectangle as shown below. In ten moves as described in the puzzle on page 62, make ten piles of two coins each. Note: Coins can move only in a straight line and cannot move diagonally.

Hint, page 110 / Answer, page 227

THE HAREM

The story goes that the harem of the great Tamerlane was protected by a door with many locks. A vizier and four slaves were in charge of guarding this door.

Knowledgeable of the weaknesses of men, Tamerlane had distributed the keys in such a way that the vizier could only open the door if he was with any one of the slaves, and the slaves could only open it if three of them worked together.

How many locks did the door have?

Hint, page 110 / Answer, page 227

THE DIVIDING END

My ID number is quite remarkable. It's a nine-digit number with each of the digits from 1 to 9 appearing once. The whole number is divisible by 9. If you remove the rightmost digit, the remaining eight-digit number is divisible by 8. Removing the next rightmost digit leaves a seven-digit number that is divisible by 7. This property continues all the way down to one digit. What is my ID number?

Hint, page 110 / Answer, page 227

THE ISLAND AND THE ENGLISHMEN

On a deserted island (except for a small group of Englishmen) there are four clubs.

The membership lists reveal that:

a) Each Englishman is a member of two clubs.

b) Every set of two clubs has only one member in common.

How many Englishmen are there on the island?

Hint, page 110 / Answer, page 228

LOGIC APPLES

Four perfect logicians, who all knew each other from being members of the Perfect Logicians' Club, sat around a table that had a dish with 11 apples in it. The chat was intense, and they ended up eating all the apples. Everybody had at least one apple, and everyone knew that fact, and each logician knew the number of apples that he ate. They didn't know how many apples each of the others ate, though. They agreed to ask only questions that they didn't know the answers to:

Alonso: Did you eat more apples than I did, Bertrand?

Bertrand: I don't know. Did you, George, eat more apples than I did?

George: I don't know.

Kurt: Aha!

Kurt figured out how many apples each person ate. Can you do the same?

Hint, page 110 / Answer, page 228

ADDED CORNERS

Using the numbers from 1 to 8, place one in each shape with one condition: The number in each square has to be the sum of its two neighboring circles.

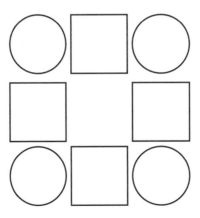

Hint, page 110 / Answer, page 228

RECTANGLES

The vertical rectangle (solid line) has an area of 40 square inches.

Find out in a quick way the area of the inclined rectangle (dotted line).

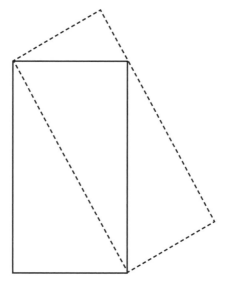

Hint, page 110 / Answer, page 229

A WARM FAREWELL

At a train station, the Porter family is saying good-bye to the Robinson family. We don't know who is leaving and who is staying.

Each of the members of the Porter family says farewell to each of the members of the Robinson family. To say good-bye, two men shake hands, and both a man and a woman and two women kiss once on the cheek.

An eyewitness to the event counted 21 handshakes and 34 kisses.

How many men and how many women were saying good-bye?

Hint, page 110 / Answer, page 229

TOUCHING SQUARES

Shown here are three squares on a table with each one touching the other two squares. If you want to place squares so that each square touches exactly three other squares (not counting corner-to-corner or corner-to-side contact), how many squares do you need? All squares must lie on the table surface.

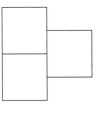

Hint, page 110 / Answer, page 229

FOUR MINUS ONE IS A CRIME

Messrs. A, B, C, and D met last night in a corner in the circled area. After the meeting, each of them went home, except for one, Mr. D, who was discovered dead this morning in the river.

"Did you take the statements from the three suspects?"

"Yes, commissioner. Mr. A declared that from the corner of the meeting he walked 7 blocks to get home. Mr. B said that he walked 6 blocks to get home. Mr. C answered that he walked 5 blocks to get home. I marked their homes on the map."

"And in which corner did they meet?"

"Nobody remembers."

"Do you want to know something? It isn't necessary, because I know that one of the three suspects is lying."

"And that is the killer!"

"Brilliant deduction!"

Who is the killer?

Hint, page 111 / Answer, page 230

ON THE ROUTE OF MARCO POLO

On his way east, Marco Polo passed five little villages along a straight road. At each village a road sign points to one of the other four villages. Below are the five signs, in no particular order. Can you add the corresponding arrows to the four signs that have lost them? (The five signs are all on the same side of the road.)

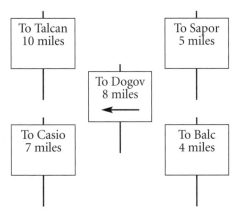

Hint, page 111 / Answer, page 230

ON THE ROAD

On my way to Philadelphia, I pass five mileposts that indicate their respective distances to Philadelphia. The mileposts are at fixed intervals. What's curious is that each milepost has a two-digit number, and together the five mileposts use all the digits from 0 to 9 once. What is the smallest distance that the closest milepost can be from Philadelphia? (As usual, mileposts don't begin with 0.)

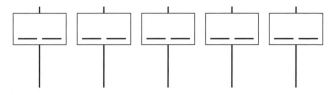

Hint, page 111 / Answer, page 230

EQUAL VISION

Each watchman looks in all directions (horizontal, vertical, and diagonal). On the left board, each watchman has five vacant cells under his gaze. (A watchman can see beyond another watchman.) On the right, each watchman can see six empty cells. What's the maximum number of watchmen that can be placed so that each sees seven empty cells?

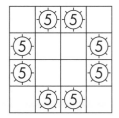 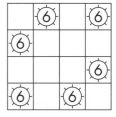

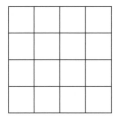

Hint, page 111 / Answer, page 231

BLOOD AND SAND

"You are the killer!" declared Commissioner Abrojos. His assistant, Inspector Begonias, slanted his eyes and looked around. They were alone in the room.

"I don't understand," he said.

"You are the killer!" the commissioner repeated.

Here is the story:

Yesterday, responding to a phone call, Inspector Begonias visited the mansion of millionaire Lincoln Dustin at around 7 P.M. The millionaire was dead in his office. There were blood stains on the carpet around the desk. Begonias inspected the place. He questioned the butler, who told him that Lincoln Dustin always led a perfectly ordered life. Every day, at noon, Mr. Dustin started the hourglass, the one that was now next to his dead body. At exactly midnight, the hourglass finished and Lincoln Dustin would go to sleep.

Begonias thought this was all very interesting, but not so useful for his investigation. That same night, the butler's call woke him up.

"Inspector!" cried the butler, "The hourglass did not finish at midnight, but at 3 A.M.!"

Begonias told all of this to Commissioner Abrojos.

"Let's suppose," said the commissioner, "that Mr. Dustin was able to turn the hourglass to leave us a clue as to the time of the crime."

Begonias nodded.

"In that case," continued the commissioner, "you told me that you had gone to the mansion around 7 P.M., which makes me think that you are the killer."

This is how they reached the conversation at the beginning of our puzzle.

Begonias could not believe it.

"I never thought," he said sadly, "that you would do this to me."

"Come on, Begonias, aren't you going to try to find an excuse?"

The inspector thought for a moment, going over the events of the previous day.

"The hourglass!" he cried. "I remember now. When I inspected the room I saw that the hourglass was on a handwritten note."

"Do you mean that the victim wrote the name of the killer? I don't believe that."

"Not at all!" said Begonias. "I wanted to read the note, so I lifted the hourglass and then I must have turned it upside down by mistake."

"What time was it then?"

"7 P.M."

"My dear friend, this clears you as a suspect!" said the commissioner.

Suppose that Mr. Dustin was able to invert the hourglass before dying. At what time did he die? Why did the commissioner consider Begonias as a suspect?

Hint, page 111 / Answer, page 231

INTERNATIONAL SUMMIT

At a recent international summit, five delegates (A, B, C, D, and E) participated. This is what we observed:

1. B and C spoke English, although when D joined them, they all changed to Spanish, the only common language among the three of them.

2. The only common language among A, B, and E was French.

3. The only common language between C and E was Italian.

4. Three delegates could speak Portuguese.

5. The most common language was Spanish.

6. One of the delegates spoke all five languages, another one spoke four, one spoke three, one spoke two, and the other only spoke one language.

What languages did each delegate speak?

Hint, page 111 / Answer, page 231

MISTER DIGIT FACE

✦ ✦ ✦

Place each of the digits 1 to 9, one digit per blank, so that the product of the two eyes equals the number above the head, and the product of each eye and mouth equals the number on the respective side of the face.

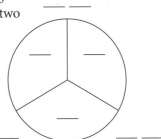

Hint, page 112 / Answer, page 233

DIGIT TREE

✦ ✦ ✦

Using each digit from 1 to 9 once, make seven numbers so that each number is equal to the sum of the numbers in the circles that are connected to it from below. (The numbers can be more than one digit.) There are two slightly different answers.

Hint, page 112 / Answer, page 233

FIGURES TO CUT IN TWO

Each one of the following figures can be divided into two equal parts (that may be mirror images of each other). The dividing lines can follow the grid or not. The grid is only to provide proportion to the figures.

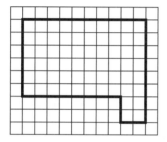

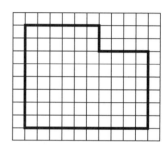

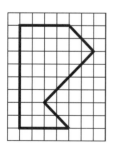

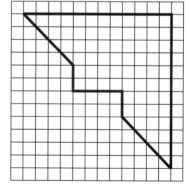

Hint, page 112 / Answer, page 234

SEGMENTS

Place the digits 1 to 9 (using each digit once, one digit per box) so that:

- the boxes containing the 1 and 2 and all the ones between them add up to 12,
- the boxes containing the 2 and 3 and all the ones between them add up to 23,
- the boxes containing the 3 and 4 and all the ones between them add up to 34,
- the boxes containing the 4 and 5 and all the ones between them add up to 45.

Hint, page 112 / Answer, page 234

MULTIPLE TOWERS

As the elevator rises along the eight-floor tower, it forms a series of three-digit numbers by combining the 72 in the elevator with the digit on the floor. What's more, these three-digit numbers are multiples of 2, 3, 4, etc., up to 9. (That is, on the lowest floor, 726 is evenly divisible by 2, on the next floor, 723 is evenly divisible by 3, and so on.) Can you find another arrangement for the digits 0 to 9 (using each digit once, one digit per box) so that the elevator isn't 72 and the combinations of the elevator with the level form an appropriate multiple?

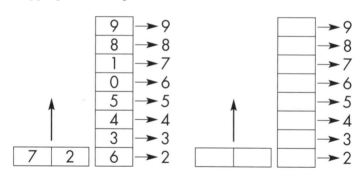

Hint, page 112 / Answer, page 235

EARTHLINGS

August 2002.

The spaceship landed.

"Earth!" they shouted.

They knew that earthlings are divided into three groups: those who always tell the truth, those who always lie, and those who do both, alternating between true and false statements, starting with either.

"Let's go!" said the captain.

The aliens approached three earthlings, who each were from a different group, and asked, "Who won the last World Cup? Who came in second? Who came in third?"

One of them responded, "Zaire first. Uruguay second. Spain third."

Another one said, "Zaire first. Spain second. Uruguay third."

The third one said, "Uruguay first. Spain second. Zaire third."

The aliens returned to their spaceship and flew back to where they came from.

Do you know which response was the true ranking in the World Cup?

Hint, page 112 / Answer, page 235

THE ANT AND THE CLOCK

Precisely when the big hand of the clock passes 12, an ant begins crawling counterclockwise around the clock from the 6 mark at a consistent speed.

When reaching the big hand of the clock, the ant turns around and, at the same speed, starts marching around the clock in the opposite direction.

Exactly 45 minutes after the first meeting, the ant crosses the big hand for the second time and dies.

How long has the ant been walking?

Hint, page 112 / Answer, page 236

HIDDEN WORD—I

A four-letter word belongs in the rectangle below. You are given several clues to help guess what it is.

In the column marked "2," you have words that share exactly two letters in the same position as the hidden word. For example, if the hidden word were REDO, in column 2 we could put DEMO, BEDS, DODO, etc. Column 1 contains words that share exactly one letter in the same position as the hidden word. In the example above, REDO being the hidden word, column 1 could have NODS, ROAD, etc.

Column 0 has words that do not share any letter in the same position as the hidden word. For our example, column 0 could have GAME, HARD, etc.

Now find the hidden word.

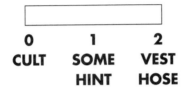

0	1	2
CULT	SOME	VEST
	HINT	HOSE

Hint, page 112 / Answer, page 237

HIDDEN WORD—II

A three-letter word belongs in the rectangle below. Given the words below, figure out what it is.

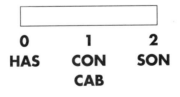

0	1	2
HAS	CON	SON
	CAB	

Hint, page 112 / Answer, page 237

HIDDEN WORD—III

A five-letter word belongs in the rectangle below. Given the words below, figure out what it is.

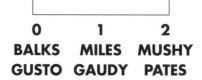

Hint, page 112 / Answer, page 237

SECRET NUMBER

In the first field of the first row of every illustration we have written (in invisible ink) a number formed by four different digits between 0 and 9.

The following rows indicate attempts to find out the secret number. Each try has, in the column to the right, its grade with letters R (right) and B (bingo). Each R indicates that this number has one digit in common with the secret number, but in a different position. Each B indicates that the number has one digit in common with the secret number in the same position.

Find out the secret number in the following tables.

SECRET NUMBER—I

				B	B	B	B
8	9	5	1	R	R		
2	1	6	9	R	B		
3	6	9	4	R	B		
4	7	2	1	R	B		
1	2	3	7	R	R	R	

Hint, page 112 / Answer, page 237

SECRET NUMBER—II

				B	B	B	B
6	2	5	3	R			
8	1	4	7	R	R		
2	5	7	1	B			
3	6	0	9	R	R		
9	6	8	7	B	B		

Hint, page 112 / Answer, page 237

SECRET NUMBER—III

				B	B	B	B
1	0	2	9	R			
3	4	6	2	R	R		
5	8	4	9	R	R		
8	5	2	1	R	R		
4	2	8	5	R	R	R	

Hint, page 112 / Answer, page 237

SECRET NUMBER—IV

				B	B	B	B
3	9	2	0	R	R	R	
8	7	4	5	B			
9	0	7	5	R	R		
8	3	9	7	R	R	R	

Hint, page 112 / Answer, page 237

SECRET NUMBER—V

				B	B	B	B
1	2	5	9	R			
1	3	8	9	R	B		
1	3	5	7	B	B		
4	3	9	7	B	B		

Hint, page 112 / Answer, page 237

DOMINOES

Each one of the following diagrams uses the 28 dominoes of a domino set to make a table. The values of each domino are written down in numbers instead of in dots, but we have not identified the individual dominoes. That's exactly what you'll have to do. In the first tables, we have helped you with some of them.

Notice that each table contains the 28 dominoes and no tile appears twice in the same table. Below each table you will find a list of the 28 dominoes so that you can track what you have found and what you are still missing.

(Dominoes was created by Mr. Lech Pijanovsky, from Poland.)

TABLE I

Find the 28 dominoes.

1	5	5	3	0	6	0	6
5	4	4	2	4	4	6	2
2	6	0	1	1	2	5	1
4	3	5	5	3	2	6	0
0	3	0	3	3	3	1	0
5	2	6	2	3	6	0	1
4	5	6	4	1	4	2	1

Here is a list of the 28 dominoes:

0-0						
0-1	1-1					
0-2	1-2	2-2				
0-3	1-3	2-3	3-3			
0-4	1-4	2-4	3-4	4-4		
0-5	1-5	2-5	3-5	4-5	5-5	
0-6	1-6	2-6	3-6	4-6	5-6	6-6

Hint, page 113 / Answer, page 238

TABLE II

Find the 28 dominoes.

3	1	2	2	6	1	3	4
5	5	3	4	0	5	3	2
2	6	5	1	1	2	0	0
1	1	0	6	0	3	3	0
0	6	4	3	6	5	4	5
3	2	5	4	0	1	6	2
5	4	6	4	2	4	6	1

Here is a list of the 28 dominoes:

0-0						
0-1	1-1					
0-2	1-2	2-2				
0-3	1-3	2-3	3-3			
0-4	1-4	2-4	3-4	4-4		
0-5	1-5	2-5	3-5	4-5	5-5	
0-6	1-6	2-6	3-6	4-6	5-6	6-6

Hint, page 113 / Answer, page 239

TABLE III

Find the 28 dominoes.

1	0	2	2	3	6	5
1	6	6	4	3	6	5
2	3	5	0	1	4	6
0	4	3	0	2	4	0
3	6	5	4	5	4	1
·0	0	5	1	3	1	2
3	6	2	2	5	3	2
1	1	4	0	4	6	5

Here is a list of the 28 dominoes:

```
0-0
0-1    1-1
0-2    1-2    2-2
0-3    1-3    2-3    3-3
0-4    1-4    2-4    3-4    4-4
0-5    1-5    2-5    3-5    4-5    5-5
0-6    1-6    2-6    3-6    4-6    5-6    6-6
```

Hint, page 113 / Answer, page 240

TABLE IV

Find the 28 dominoes.

5	4	2	3	6	3	4
4	6	5	5	0	6	3
4	6	2	3	4	1	2
6	0	6	3	0	4	1
0	6	0	2	3	4	2
5	5	6	1	4	5	3
5	1	3	2	2	1	1
1	5	2	0	1	0	0

Here is a list of the 28 dominoes:

```
0-0
0-1   1-1
0-2   1-2   2-2
0-3   1-3   2-3   3-3
0-4   1-4   2-4   3-4   4-4
0-5   1-5   2-5   3-5   4-5   5-5
0-6   1-6   2-6   3-6   4-6   5-6   6-6
```

Hint, page 113 / Answer, page 241

TABLE V

Find the 28 dominoes.

4	0	0	1	1	1	0
5	2	3	5	6	5	6
3	5	4	4	3	4	2
2	0	0	5	6	5	3
2	2	1	5	6	0	1
2	4	4	3	2	6	4
5	6	0	3	2	3	6
1	1	3	6	4	1	0

Here is a list of the 28 dominoes:

```
0-0
0-1   1-1
0-2   1-2   2-2
0-3   1-3   2-3   3-3
0-4   1-4   2-4   3-4   4-4
0-5   1-5   2-5   3-5   4-5   5-5
0-6   1-6   2-6   3-6   4-6   5-6   6-6
```

Hint, page 113 / Answer, page 242

TABLE VI

Find the 28 dominoes.

4	5	1	6	0	5	1
2	5	3	5	3	6	5
6	2	0	4	2	2	6
6	6	2	0	5	3	3
3	1	1	2	3	6	4
4	0	3	1	0	0	4
4	1	2	1	4	5	3
5	1	2	0	0	4	6

Here is a list of the 28 dominoes:

0-0						
0-1	1-1					
0-2	1-2	2-2				
0-3	1-3	2-3	3-3			
0-4	1-4	2-4	3-4	4-4		
0-5	1-5	2-5	3-5	4-5	5-5	
0-6	1-6	2-6	3-6	4-6	5-6	6-6

Hint, page 113 / Answer, page 243

HOUND—I

A hound started on a square numbered 1, and moved from square to square numbering them in succession to the last one, numbered 20. The hound moved horizontally and vertically only, never entering any square twice. The numbers were then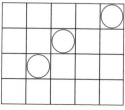
deleted. All we know is that the squares with circles had the numbers 5, 10, and 15, in some order. Figure out the path of the hound.

Hint, page 113 / Answer, page 244

HOUND—II

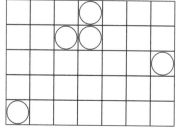
A hound started on a square numbered 1, and moved from square to square numbering them in succession to the last one, numbered 35. The hound moved horizontally and vertically only, never entering any square twice. The numbers were then deleted. All we know is that the squares with circles had the numbers 7, 14, 21, 28, and 35, in some order. Figure out the path of the hound.

Hint, page 113 / Answer, page 244

HOUND—III

A hound started on a square numbered 1, and moved from square to square numbering them in succession to the last one, numbered 25. The hound never entered any square twice and moved horizontally and vertically only, except for one diagonal move to a neighboring square. All the numbers except those shown were then deleted. Figure out the path of the hound.

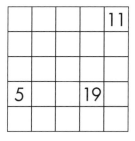

Hint, page 113/ Answer, page 245

HOUND—IV

A hound started on a square numbered 1, and moved from square to square numbering them in succession to the last one, numbered 25. The hound never entered any square twice and moved horizontally and vertically only, except for one jump move like a chess knight, shown below left. All the numbers except those shown were then deleted. Figure out the path of the hound.

	16			
				10
			20	
	3	19		

Hint, page 113 / Answer, page 245

HOUND—V

A hound started on a square numbered 1, and moved from square to square numbering them in succession to the last one, numbered 9. The hound never entered any square twice and moved horizontally and vertically only. The prime numbers in the grid formed a symmetric pattern. Figure out the path of the hound in the bigger board where the prime numbers (2, 3, 5, 7, 11, 13, 17, 19, and 23) form a symmetric pattern. One number has been supplied. There are two answers.

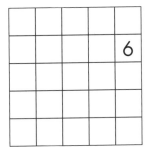

Hint, page 113 / Answer, page 246

POKER

We have a set of 28 poker cards (with 8, 9, 10, J, Q, K, and A). We select 25 and make a five-by-five table, like in the drawings.

We then have twelve "hands" of five cards (five horizontally, five vertically, and two diagonally). Next to each "hand" we write its combination.

Pair: two cards of the same value.

Two pair: two pairs plus a fifth card.

Three of a kind: three cards of equal value.

Full house: three of a kind with a pair.

Four of a kind: four cards of the same value.

Straight: five cards of consecutive values. The ace can be high or low, so the possible combinations of a straight are: A-8-9-10-J, 8-9-10-J-Q, 9-10-J-Q-K, and 10-J-Q-K-A.

Straight flush: a straight where all cards are of the same suit.

(We write "nothing" when we have none of these combinations.)

Important: The cards of each "hand" do not have to be in order. For example, the line containing the straight can have a 9, then an 8, then a J, then a 10, then an A.

Find the values (just the values, not the suits) of all cards left blank.

POKER—I

◆ ◆ ◆

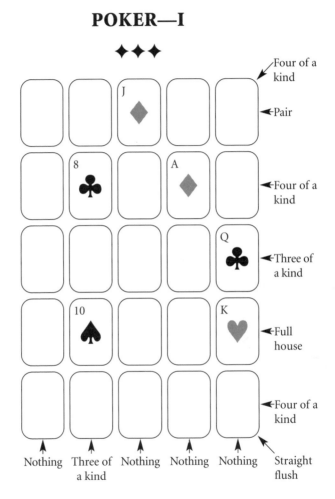

Four of a kind

Pair

Four of a kind

Three of a kind

Full house

Four of a kind

Nothing   Three of a kind   Nothing   Nothing   Nothing   Straight flush

Hint, page 113 / Answer, page 247

POKER—II

♦ ♦ ♦

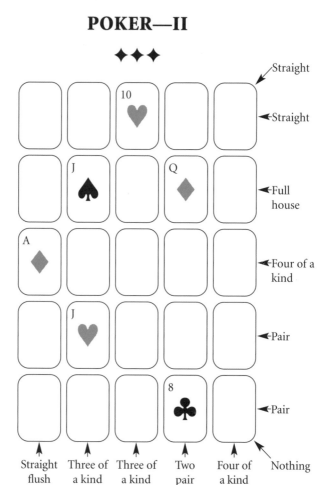

Hint, page 113 / Answer, page 248

POKER—III

♦ ♦ ♦

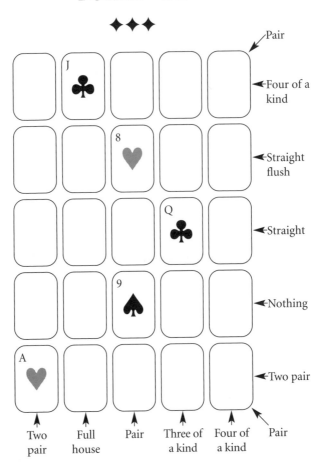

Hint, page 113 / Answer, page 249

POKER—IV

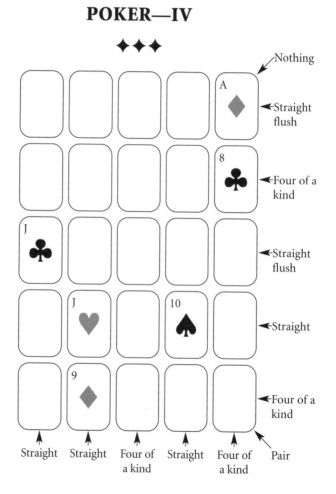

Hint, page 113 / Answer, page 250

POKER—V

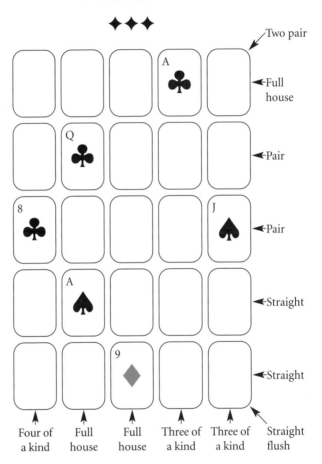

Hint, page 113 / Answer, page 251

POKER—VI

♦ ♦ ♦

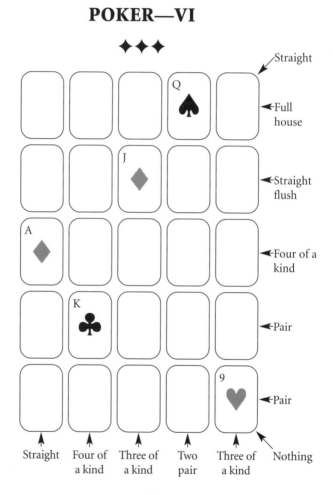

Hint, page 113 / Answer, page 252

HINTS

Here are clues to help solve the problems.

TWINS (page 44). If a person always lies or always tells the truth, can he call himself a liar?

TWIN STATISTICS (page 44). Imagine there are 100 births, with 3% being twin births. How many people are born?

PLACE YOUR CARDS (page 44). Place the diamond by following the first clue given in the puzzle. You can now tell what the queen's suit is.

THE PROFESSOR AND HIS FRIEND (page 45). Did you notice that each player takes an odd number of matches?

IRREGULAR CIRCUIT (page 46). Why not take the first pass as a new starting point?

ECONOMICAL PROGRESSION (page 47). The three digits are 1, 2, and 6.

SKIN AND SHOES (page 47). Look at one foot and count the rest.

EVE'S ENIGMA (page 48). The snake tells Eve that today is Saturday and tomorrow is Wednesday. Isn't that odd? On what days of the week can the snake talk like that?

WHAT MONTH—I (page 48). It must be a strange month, right?

WHAT MONTH—II (page 49). Note that 38 is a very high number for the sum of the first Thursday of a month and of the last Monday of another month. What days could give such a high result?

UP AND DOWN (page 49). The professor had an advantage of 11 steps and is climbing at twice my speed.

BROKEN M (page 50). It might be useful to draw three straight lines on a white piece of paper and then draw an M on top of them.

SOCCER SCORES—I (page 51). How many games were played in the tournament? How many points in total were there in the entire tournament?

SOCCER SCORES—II (page 51). What were the scores for the games played by the Lions? What were the scores for the Bears?

PROHIBITED CONNECTION (page 52). Notice that the number 1 can be connected with five other digits. This does not occur for 2, 3, 4, or 5.

WHAT TIME IS IT, I–IV (pages 52–53). Think of a time, say, 3 o'clock. Are the conditions of the problem true for the time you just thought of? In what area of the clock are we closer to the conditions of the puzzle?

CONCENTRIC (page 54). Move the figure. What happens when you rotate the small square?

JOHN CASH (page 54). When John erased the first number, there was a two-digit number left. Think about it. If you remove the number in the tens column, this two-digit number is divided by five.

NEW RACE (page 55). Take A as the starting point.

RUSSIAN ROULETTE (page 56). By the first answer you know that the snuff/salt pair is vertical. Can it be on the right side? Remember that a jar never contains the ingredient shown on the label.

THE CALCULATOR KEYS (page 57). This puzzle has two solutions. Give it a try.

NICE DISCOUNTS (page 58). Buy all the books in just two days.

HOROSCOPE (page 58). Without doubt, this is a very special date.

ENIGMATIC FARES (page 59). The tickets have consecutive numbers. The sum of the digits of both is 62, an even number. What is the last digit of the first ticket?

MONTE CARLO (page 59). Let's say that you start with $100. If you lose and win, what happens to your money?

STRANGERS IN THE NIGHT (page 60). There are exactly four true statements. Only one person is guilty. What does this mean about the "I'm innocent" statements?

THE FOREIGNERS AND THE MENU (page 61). Out of the five dishes they order each night, could it be that two of them are the same?

FORT KNOX JUMPING FROGS, I–V (pages 62–66). Play with some coins.

THE HAREM (page 67). Try it. If the door had 3 locks, could Tamerlane's system work?

THE DIVIDING END (page 67). Let's call the ID number ABCDEFGHI. ABCDE can be divided evenly by 5, so we know what E is.

THE ISLAND AND THE ENGLISHMEN (page 68). Draw 4 circles that represent the clubs. Connect the clubs to the members.

LOGIC APPLES (page 68). Alonso would not have asked the question if he had eaten 5 or more apples, because nobody could have eaten more than him.

ADDED CORNERS (page 69). Place the 8 first. Can it be in a corner?

RECTANGLES (page 70). Find a simple way to divide the figure.

A WARM FAREWELL (page 71). Add the number of handshakes and kisses. It comes to a total of 55. If each Porter said good-bye to each Robinson, the number of the Porter family members multiplied by the number of the Robinson family members must equal 55.

TOUCHING SQUARES (page 71). You'll need more than 10 squares.

FOUR MINUS ONE IS A CRIME (page 72). Go from A to B on the map. Try different routes. Count how many blocks you travel every time. Compare it with the suspects' statements.

ON THE ROUTE OF MARCO POLO (page 73). Each sign points to a different village. What can be said of the sum of the distances in each direction?

ON THE ROAD (page 74). From one sign to the next the tens' column must change.

EQUAL VISION (page 75). It can be done with three or four watchmen. Can you do it with more?

BLOOD AND SAND (page 76). Why did the commissioner suspect Begonias? Put yourself in his shoes. You do not know that Begonias inverted the hourglass, but instead you believe that Lincoln Dustin did it when dying.

INTERNATIONAL SUMMIT (page 78). Use the table below. B and C speak English. Put an X in rows B and C in the English column. D doesn't speak English. Put an O in the D row in the English column.

	Eng.	Sp.	Fr.	Port.	Ital.
A					
B	X				
C	X				
D	O				
E					

MISTER DIGIT FACE (page 79). Where can 9 go?

DIGIT TREE (page 79). With the nine digits we have to make 7 numbers. Two numbers will have two digits each. What is the highest number that could be at the top of the tree?

FIGURES TO CUT IN TWO (page 80). Try several times. There is no definite way. It's a matter of eyesight.

SEGMENTS (page 81). The sum of all nine digits is 45.

MULTIPLE TOWERS (page 82). Certain levels must have even numbers.

EARTHLINGS (page 83). The second earthling had one answer in common with the first one and one in common with the third. Is this earthling honest, a liar, or both?

THE ANT AND THE CLOCK (page 84). Draw a clock. Draw the path of the ant. Compare distances.

HIDDEN WORD, I–III (pages 84–86). Compare the words in column 0 with the others. If one letter appears in the same position in column 0 and also in another, you can cross it out in that column, since you know it will not be in the word in the rectangle.

SECRET NUMBER, I–V (pages 86–89). When you know that a digit is not in the secret number, cross it out. If you discover that a digit is in the secret number, but don't know where, circle it. When you find its correct position, mark it with a square. Do this for all lines. Make a list of the digits that are definitely in the secret number, another for those that are not in the secret number, and a third list for those you are not sure about.

DOMINOES, I–VI (pages 89–95). Cross out the dominoes that are already placed in the list. Let's imagine that the domino 3-4 has already been placed. Separate every other instance of 3 and 4 together in the table (remember, dominoes only appear once). Then look for pairs of numbers that are together (like 5 and 6, for example) and do the same. As you go from one puzzle to the next, you will think of more strategies.

HOUND—I (page 96). If you think of the distances between the marked squares you can place the number 10. Think of where the odd and even numbers go.

HOUND—II (page 96). The lower left box is 21.

HOUND—III (page 97). The lower left box is 25.

HOUND—IV (page 98). The lower left box is 1.

HOUND—V (page 99). We have 9 prime numbers. To obtain a symmetric figure, we must have the same quantity of prime numbers on the left as on the right.

If we paint the board like a checkerboard with a black diagonal, we will have 12 white squares and 13 black ones. Where do the prime numbers go?

POKER, I–VI (pages 100–106). The straight combinations are the most useful information for you at first, especially the straight flushes. Four of a kind is also useful. Remember that all straights must have a 10 and a J, and that a four of a kind has four cards of equal value. If for a certain card you have two possible values, consider each value individually until you find the solution.

BRAIN BAFFLERS

1. GUESS THE THEME–I
✦✦✦

A, B, C, and D each represent a different word or phrase, and they have a common theme. What are the four words or phrases and what is the theme?

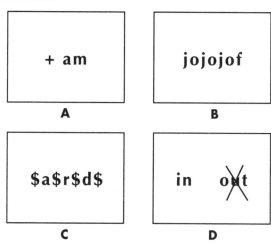

Answer, page 254

2. MISSING NUMBER–I
✦✦✦

What is the missing number?

9   22   24   12   __   4   13

Answer, page 254

3. LATERAL SHAPES

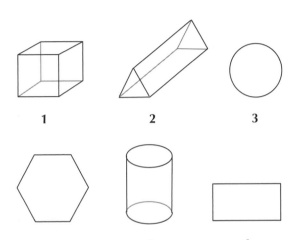

Thinking laterally, which of the following are the seventh and eighth shapes in the series above?

Answer, page 254

4. FIND THE NUMBER–I

Find a ten-digit number that:
- can be described as having m digits between the m's, n digits between the n's, and so on, and
- whose first digit is a prime number, the two-digit number formed by its second and third digits is a prime number, the three-digit number formed by its fourth, fifth, and sixth digits is three times a prime number, and the four-digit number formed by its last four digits is also a prime number.

Answer, page 254

5. HORSESHOE

How can a horseshoe be cut into six pieces with two straight cuts? There are three different ways.

Answer, page 254

6. GUESS THE THEME–II
♦ ♦ ♦

A, B, C, and D each represent a different word or phrase, and they have a common theme. What are the four words or phrases and what is the theme?

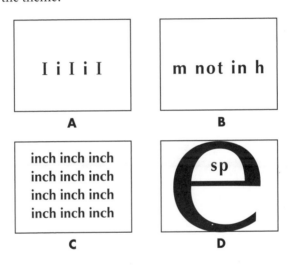

A

B

C

D

Answer, page 255

7. SECRET CODE
♦ ♦ ♦

If W = 2, U = 4, V = 5, G = 8, and Y = 20, what does D equal?

Answer, page 255

8. PHRASE GRID–I

What two-word phrase could form the first and fourth rows of the diagram so that each column contains a four-letter word?

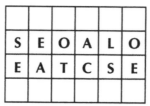

Answer, page 255

9. WORD GRID–I

Complete the grid using all the letters below so that each row and column containing two or more squares is a word when read from left to right or from top to bottom.

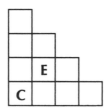

A D E F I N S T

Answer, page 255

10. SOCCER TOURNAMENT

In an international soccer tournament, the scores in a certain round were as follows:

Argentina	0	**N. Ireland**	0
Belgium	1	**Wales**	4
England	0	**Scotland**	1
France	1	**Spain**	2
Germany	1	**Brazil**	1
Italy	3	**Denmark**	1
Peru	2	**Cameroon**	0
Poland	?	**Portugal**	?

Each score is related to the name of the corresponding country. Crack the code to figure out what the score was in the final match.

Answer, page 255

11. MISSING LEAF

One leaf has been torn out of a book. The sum of the remaining page numbers is 10,000. What is the last-numbered page in the book, and which leaf is missing?

Answer, page 255

12. CROSSWORD ANAGRAMS–I

♦ ♦ ♦

Each of these crossword clues is a full anagram of the answer:

ACROSS

2. I hire parsons (12)
3. On tip (5)
4. Date's up (4,3)
5. Is a lane (2,5)
6. Here come dots (3,5,4)
7. Eleven + two (6+3)
8. Must anger (9)

DOWN

1. No untidy clothes (3,6,6)

Answer, page 255

13. GUESS THE THEME–III
✦✦✦

A, B, C, and D each represent a different word or phrase, and they have a common theme. What are the four words or phrases and what is the theme?

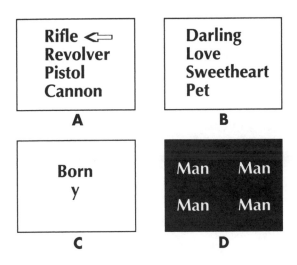

Answer, page 256

14. WORDPLAY–I

The answer to the first of these is "29 days in February in a leap year." Complete the rest.

29 D in F in a L Y

12 S of the Z

7 W of the A W

54 C in a D (with the J)

32 D F, at which W F

18 H on a G C

4 Q in a G

14 P in a S

Answer, page 256

15. FIND THE NUMBER–II

Find a four-digit number that is equal to the square of the sum of the number formed by its first two digits and the number formed by its last two digits, and is exactly 1,000 different from another four-digit number with the same property.

Answer, page 256

16. ROW HOUSES

There are five men in five houses. Each man comes from a different town (all genuine names), has a different pet, and supports a different rugby team. From the following clues, determine which man supports the Waratahs and, if different, which man has a kea.

1. The five houses are in a row and each is a different color.
2. The man who has the kangaroo lives next to the man from Woy Woy.
3. Mr. Brown supports the Brumbies.
4. The man from Wagga Wagga lives in the blue house.
5. Mr. Green lives in the mauve house.
6. The man from Bong Bong has a kookaburra.
7. Mr. White comes from Aka Aka.
8. Mr. Gray lives on the left in the first house.
9. The red house is to the right of and adjacent to the yellow house.
10. The man from Peka Peka supports the Hurricanes.
11. The man who has a koala lives next door to the man from Wagga Wagga.
12. Mr. Black has a kiwi.
13. The man in the middle house supports the Sharks.
14. The man in the red house supports the Crusaders.
15. The maroon house is next to Mr. Gray's house.

Answer, page 256

17. GUESS THE THEME–IV

A, B, C, and D each represent a different word or phrase, and they
have a common theme. What are the four words or phrases and
what is the theme?

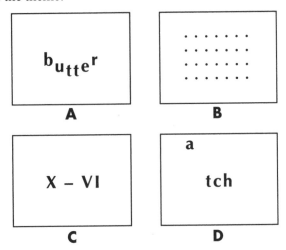

Answer, page 256

18. TENNIS BALLS

Tennis is a sport in which you can you take a container that is half
full of balls, add another ball, and still have a container that is half
full. True or false?

Answer, page 256

19. ALPHABET?

Two lists of words have been created. Embedded in one list are the 26 letters of the alphabet in their correct order. Embedded in the other list are the 26 letters of the alphabet in reverse order.

The alphabet (forward or backward, as appropriate) has been removed from each list, and the spaces between words have been closed up. In each case the following letters remain:

DOEBOSITELEROEUIUSIGUATGLIEAEST

All the words in the original two lists have at least three letters, and each word in each list includes at least one letter from the above string and at least one letter of the alphabet that was subsequently removed.

Find two lists of words—one containing the 26 letters of the alphabet in their correct order and the second containing the 26 letters in reverse alphabetical order—that meet these conditions.

Answer, page 256

20. U.S.A. GEOGRAPHY

Although this puzzle seems easy when you hear the answer, few people are able to get all four answers right the first time. In fact, three out of four can be considered a very good score. Name the northernmost, southernmost, easternmost, and westernmost states of the U.S.A.

Answer, page 257

21. TOURISTS' MEALS

The Golden Bay Dining Tour itinerary includes six dinners. Five tourists following this itinerary are all at different stages of the tour. One tourist has dined once so far, and the other four have dined two, three, four, and five times. The dining itinerary begins and ends with dinner at The Old School Cafe, and the four dinners between are at four other restaurants and always in the same order.

From this information and the information below, determine where each tourist comes from, the name of the restaurant at which the tourist last dined, and the name of the restaurant at which the tourist will be dining next.

1. Ann, who is not from Christchurch, will dine next at the Farewell Spit Cafe.

2. Ben does not come from Auckland.

3. Cathy, who last dined at Milliways Restaurant, will not be dining at the Collingwood Tavern next.

4. David is not from Auckland or Dunedin, and dined last at somewhere other than the Collingwood Tavern.

5. Emma comes from Hamilton.

6. The next person to dine at the Wholemeal Cafe did not last dine at the Collingwood Tavern.

7. Ben, the person from Christchurch, the person who last dined at the Farewell Spit Cafe, and the person who will next dine at Milliways Restaurant are four of the five tourists.

8. Neither the person from Wellington nor the person from Dunedin will be dining next at the Collingwood Tavern.

Answer, page 257

22. GUESS THE THEME–V
✦✦✦

A, B, C, and D each represent a different word or phrase, and they have a common theme. What are the four words or phrases and what is the theme?

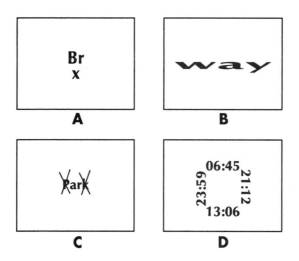

Answer, page 257

23. CROSSWORD ANAGRAMS–II

Each of these crossword clues is a full anagram of the answer:

ACROSS

1. Stopped? No (9)
3. The or (5)
4. Moon starer (10)
5. Name for ship (3,8)
6. Tender names (11)

7. Has to pilfer (1,10)
8. They see (3,4)

DOWN

2. No city dust here (3,11)

Answer, page 257

24. CALENDAR CUBES

A calendar comprises a stand and two printed cubes. Each day both cubes are positioned in the stand to read the day's date, which can of course be any number from 01 to 31. How are the numbers arranged on the cubes?

Answer, page 257

25. NUMBER COLUMNS

The first ten natural numbers have been arranged into columns according to a certain rule, as shown below:

1	4	3
2	5	7
6	9	8
10		

A. The numbers 11 and 12 would appear in the same column as each other, but which one?

B. If the arrangement were continued indefinitely, what would be the final entry in the third column?

Answer, page 258

26. GUESS THE THEME–VI
✦✦✦

A, B, C, and D each represent a different word or phrase, and they have a common theme. What are the four words or phrases and what is the theme?

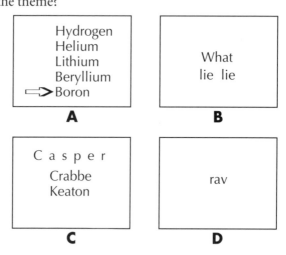

Answer, page 258

27. UNUSUAL?
✦✦✦

Although at first you may not think so, this paragraph is unusual. A quick study will show that it has capitals, commas, and full stops so that punctuation, as far as I know, is satisfactory. But this paragraph is most unusual, and I would hazard my opinion that you do not know why. Should you look at it backwards, or in a mirror, or both, you will find just rubbish, so obviously that is not a way to a solution. Ability at crosswords and similar things may assist you, but I doubt it. If you still do not know what this paragraph is all about, you could go back and start again, but you should not find it particularly difficult. I warn you to watch for your sanity though, as this paragraph is unnatural. Can you work out why? Good luck!

Answer, page 258

28. MAGIC HEXAGON
✦ ✦ ✦

Place the numbers from 1 to 19 in the diagram in such a way that the numbers in each of the 15 straight lines of small hexagons have the same total, namely 38. It is not easy, but it can be done!

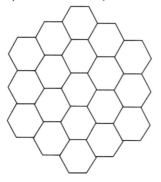

Answer, page 258

29. PRIME SECURITY

Security at Prime Palace is a very straightforward affair. There are no keys, just simple bracelets on which are hung five numbers. Access to sensitive areas is then granted by presenting the bracelet in a way that shows a five-digit prime number. Given that a bracelet can be read clockwise or counterclockwise and there are five numbers to start from, the chances of picking a prime number at random can therefore be as low as one in ten.

Sounds simple? Well, as an extra check, you are asked to swap your bracelet for one of the same color at every door, so you need to know for your color the full set of possible prime numbers.

Although the system worked well for many years, it was almost abandoned when the queen remarried. The new king simply could not remember his numbers! He therefore was given a special bracelet that always produced a prime however it was presented, and he was never asked to swap bracelets.

What numbers were on the king's bracelet?

Answer, page 258

30. PRIME SECURITY–II

Prime Palace (see puzzle 29 above) now wants to move to a six-figure system. Will there be a suitable new bracelet for the king?

Answer, page 258

31. GUESS THE THEME–VII

A, B, C, and D each represent a different word or phrase, and they have a common theme. What are the four words or phrases and what is the theme?

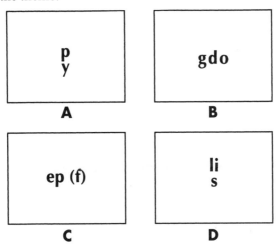

Answer, page 259

32. COUNTRY Q & Z
♦ ♦ ♦

The name of which country includes both a "q" and a "z"?

Answer, page 259

33. WORD SEARCH CONSTRUCTION

Readers are no doubt familiar with "word search" puzzles, where various (usually related) words are hidden in an array and the puzzle is simply to find them. The words may run horizontally, vertically, or diagonally, may run in either direction, or may overlap, but they must run in a straight line. Often there are letters in the array that are not used.

Construct a word search puzzle using the words ONE, TWO, THREE, FOUR, FIVE, SIX, SEVEN, EIGHT, NINE, TEN, ELEVEN, and TWELVE in the grid below.

When completed, the diagram below will have just one unused letter.

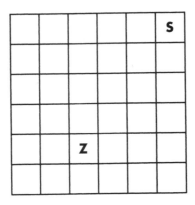

Answer, page 259

34. SOLITAIRE BOARD

Zoe's solitaire board consists of 28 holes set out in a triangle as shown in the diagram. The game starts with a peg in every hole except the central one (shaded in the diagram) and is played in the usual way. Each move consists of jumping a peg over an adjacent peg into a hole, with the peg over which the jump is made then being removed from the board. The aim is to be left with only one peg on the board.

Through trial and error, Zoe has convinced herself that the puzzle is impossible. Can you help her prove this?

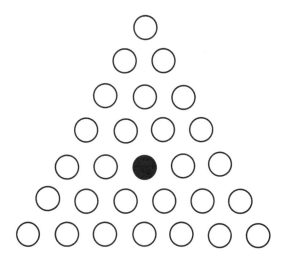

Answer, page 259

35. GUESS THE THEME–VIII

A, B, C, and D each represent a different word or phrase, and they have a common theme. What are the four words or phrases and what is the theme?

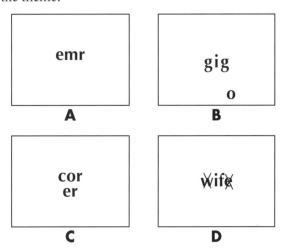

Answer, page 260

36. ALPHABETICAL ORDER?
◆◆◆

Can it be said that the six words below are in alphabetical order?

almost   belt   dirt   know   jot   most

Answer, page 260

37. XSUM

X and XSUM are two variables related to each other as follows:

XSUM equals the total of the digits comprising X
X equals (XSUM)³

One solution is XSUM = 8 and X = 512, where XSUM as well as X is a cube. Trivial solutions where XSUM as well as X are cubes are X = XSUM = 0 and X = XSUM = 1. Given that there is one more solution where XSUM is a cube than when XSUM is not a cube, how many solutions are there?

Answer, page 260

38. CARPENTER CUTS

A carpenter has a solid cube of wood, each edge of which is twelve inches long. He wishes to cut the block in two in such a way that the new face on each of the two pieces can then be trimmed to a square of maximum possible size. Where should he make the cut?

Answer, page 260

39. FAMILY TREE

What were the relationships of the people mentioned in the following epitaph?

Two husbands with their two wives
Two grandmothers with their two granddaughters
Two fathers with their two daughters
Two mothers with their two sons
Two maidens with their two mothers
Two sisters with their two brothers
But only six in all lie buried here
All born legitimate, from incest clear.

Answer, page 260

40. COUNTRY ANAGRAMS

Each word in the following list is an anagram of a country, but with one letter changed. For example, "least" would lead to "Wales," with "w" replaced by "t." What are the countries?

1. empty
2. tiara
3. tribal
4. warden

5. amenity
6. elegant
7. glacier
8. senator

Answer, page 261

41. WORD CIRCLES–I
✦✦✦

What three letters should be placed in the three empty circles in order that the longest possible word (which may be more than eight letters long) can be spelled out by reading around the circles? You can choose your starting position and whether to read the letters clockwise or counterclockwise.

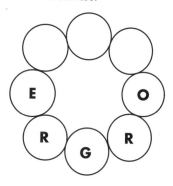

Answer, page 261

42. MATH CLASS
✦✦✦

Jimmy learned in school that $1^2 + 2^2 = 5$ and $3^2 + 4^2 = 5^2$. Hurrying to do his homework, he writes, $1^3 + 2^3 + 3^3 = 6^2$ and then $3^3 + 4^3 + 5^3 = 6^3$. Was he right?

Answer, page 261

43. Xs & Os
✦✦✦

Divide the following figure into four parts, with each part being the same size and shape and comprising whole squares only. Each of the four parts should also contain one X and one O, though not necessarily in the same relative positions.

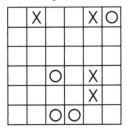

Answer, page 261

44. LETTERS FOR DIGITS–I
✦✦✦

In the equation below, each letter represents one digit only, and no letter represents the same digit as any other letter:

TIM x SOLE = AMOUNT

Furthermore, and using the same letters to represent the same digits, the difference between LEAST and MOST is ALL. In this puzzle a number may begin with zero; such a zero should be ignored when performing calculations. What digits do the letters stand for?

Answer, page 261

45. GUESS THE THEME–IX

A, B, C, and D each represent a different word or phrase, and they have a common theme. What are the four words or phrases and what is the theme?

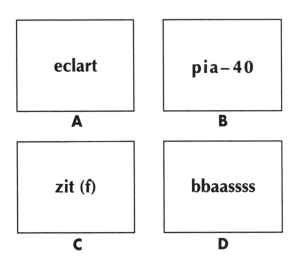

Answer, page 262

46. TRIANGULAR ANGLES

Triangle OAB is formed by three tangents to a circle with center C. Angle AOB = 40°. What is angle ACB?

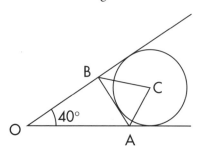

Answer, page 262

47. MATHEMATICAL 4'S–I
✦✦✦

Using four 4's, parentheses as necessary, and the following seven symbols as required, find expressions for 73 and 89.

The use of nonstandard expressions such as .($\sqrt{4}$) for 0.2 or ($\sqrt{\sqrt{\sqrt{\sqrt{\sqrt{....\sqrt{\sqrt{4}}}}}}}$) for 1 is not permitted.

Answer, page 263

48. CROSSWORD PUZZLING

✦✦✦

A crossword puzzle with some puzzling clues:

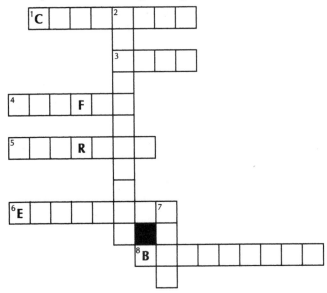

ACROSS

1. A kettle called Ronald (8)
3. Divide or add to make her shorter (4)
4. A word that is an anagram of itself (6)
5. An American film actress from Germany (3,4)

6. Contains the letter "e" three times, but often seen containing just one letter (8)
8. ONMLKJIH (9)

DOWN

2. A rope ends it (11)
7. Cheese made backwards (4)

Answer, page 263

49. GUESS THE THEME–X

A, B, C, and D each represent a different word or phrase, and they have a common theme. What are the four words or phrases and what is the theme?

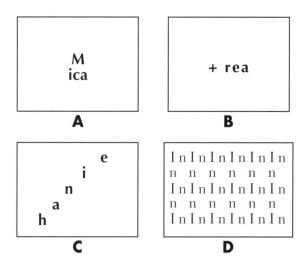

Answer, page 263

50. ARMY RIDER

An army four miles long steadily advances four miles while a dispatch rider gallops from the rear to the front, delivers a dispatch to the commanding general as he turns, and gallops back to the rear. How far has the rider traveled?

Answer, page 263

51. SEVEN IN A ROW

"Catchphrase" has six consonants in a row and does not have a y. Find a word that starts with seven consonants in a row, counting y as a consonant, and ends with nine.

Answer, page 263

52. NATIVE LAND

If Alan is from New Zealand,

And Britain's where Rita is from,

Please tell me if you are so able,

The countries of Eric and Don?

Answer, page 264

53. LETTERS FOR DIGITS–II

THIS ✗ THAT ✗ IT equals a ten-digit number containing each digit once. If each letter represents a different digit, and **THAT** is a perfect square, what is **THIS**?

Answer, page 264

54. MISSING LETTER

What is the missing letter below?

E O E R E X ? T E N

Answer, page 264

55. POSTAL HOLE
✦✦✦

The hole for letters in the pillar-box at our local post office is rectangular and wider than it is high. Each side of the hole is an integral number of inches in length, and the area of the hole in square inches is 25 percent greater than the perimeter in inches. What is the width of the hole?

Answer, page 264

56. FIND THE NUMBER–III
✦✦✦

Find an eight-digit number containing eight different digits that is equal to the square of the sum of the number formed by its first four digits and the number formed by its last four digits.

Answer, page 264

57. FIND THE NUMBER–IV
✦✦✦

Jill has thought of a number between 13 and 1,300, and Jack is doing his best to guess it. Unknown to Jack, Jill is not always truthful.

Jack asks whether the number is below 500.	Jill lies.
Jack asks whether the number is a perfect square.	Jill lies.
Jack asks whether the number is a perfect cube.	Jill tells the truth.
Jack then asks whether the second digit is a zero.	Jill answers.

Jack then states the number that he thinks Jill thought of and, not surprisingly, is wrong. From the information above, name Jill's number.

Answer, page 264

58. LUNCH BREAK BOOKS

At work, Alan, Ben, Claire, Dave, Emma, Fiona, Gail, and Henry have their lunch break together. Their lunchroom has four tables against a wall, each for two people.

They decided to have a quiz week where they would each read puzzles over lunch from their favorite puzzle book. In alphabetical order, the eight favorite puzzle books, one per person, were: *Brain Bafflers*, *Crosswords*, *Cryptograms*, *Logic Puzzles*, *Mazes*, *Number Games*, *Probability Paradoxes*, and *Word Search*.

In that week, no two people sat together at lunch more than once. Given that they all lunched together every day unless stated otherwise, determine each person's favorite puzzle book.

Monday

Alan sat beside the reader of *Number Games*.

The *Crosswords* reader was on a diet and skipped the lunch break.

Tuesday

The *Word Search* reader sat beside Gail, and Ben sat beside Emma.

In the evening, Claire left for a week's holiday.

Wednesday

Dave sat beside the *Word Search* reader.

Fiona was ill and so did not go to work that day.

The *Brain Bafflers* reader sat beside Alan, who is not the reader of *Word Search*.

Thursday

The *Mazes* reader was away on business in the morning and missed lunch.

Alan and Emma sat together.

The woman whose favorite puzzle book is *Cryptograms* sat beside Dave.

Friday

Ben took the day off.

Fiona and Dave sat together.

Saturday

The readers of *Number Games* and *Logic Puzzles* sat together.

Answer, page 265

59. SCHOOL ENROLLMENT

Two pupils were to be chosen at random from a school register to take part in a competition. The probability that both would be boys was one-third. Before the choice could be made however, a decision was taken to include pupils from the register of another school in the ballot for the two places. This other school had a register of 1,000 pupils, and the chance that the two selected pupils would both be boys was reduced to one-thirteenth.

How many pupils are on the register of the first school?

Answer, page 265

60. GUESS THE THEME–XI

A, B, C, and D each represent a different word or phrase, and they have a common theme. What are the four words or phrases and what is the theme?

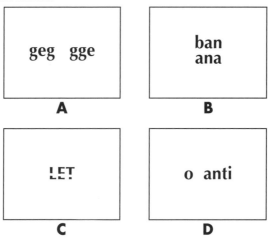

Answer, page 265

61. NO PUNCTUATION
✦✦✦

Punctuate the following so that it makes sense:

Time flies you cannot they go too quickly

Answer, page 265

62. CHESS–I

✦✦✦

Construct a chess game in which White moves one piece twice and opens with 1. P— KB3 (see diagram), and Black mates on move five with 5. . . . . N x R mate using his king's knight.

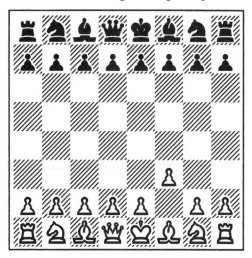

Answer, page 266

63. CHESS–II

✦✦✦

This is the same as the previous puzzle, but this time the mate in five is with Black's queen's knight.

Answer, page 266

64. PICK-A-WORD CROSSWORD

Each clue in this crossword leads to two words that are anagrams of each other. For example, the clue "Drums like the Concorde" would give PERCUSSION/SUPERSONIC. Use interlocking letters to determine which word is to be entered in the diagram.

ACROSS

7. Least colorful parts of a flower (6)
8. Confident save (6)
9. Very odd place for hot coals (7)
11. Subsequently change (5)
12. Provide food for a very small quantity (5)
14. Dependent upon where one finds a relieved soldier? (7)
15. Fired for trying to lose pounds (7)
17. Express reaches the top (5)
20. Applauds the top of the head (5)
21. Place: the upper part (7)
23. Removes more than one case of spots (6)
24. Slip away in a dreamy state (6)

DOWN

1. A type of paper tiger say (6)
2. Sat down and composed (6)
3. Skills of leading performer (4)
4. Enlarge a small part (6)
5. Most impertinent piece of baggage (8)
6. Got to know regular payment (6)
10. Made furious (7)
13. Produce an adolescent, possibly (8)
15. Came out of obsolescence (6)
16. Make known it may be sweaty (6)
18. Pet dog doubled back (6)
19. Tolerates having prejudice (6)
22. Cheese and wine (4)

Answer, page 267

65. CROSSNUMBERS–I

Each number from 90 to 99 has been expressed as the product or quotient of two positive integers, neither of which is 1. Each of these integers has, in turn, been expressed as a combination of two integers, and it is these that appear in the diagram below. No number in the diagram begins with 0, and no number appears twice. Capital letters denote "across" numbers, and lowercase letters denote "down" numbers.

A	a	b	B	c	Cd		D	e	f
Eg		F	h	G			Hi		
I		j	J		K	k			l
	m	L		n	Mo		N	p	
Oq			P			Q	r	R	
S			T		U		V		

$$90 = (A - n) \cdot (H / a)$$
$$91 = (e / E) \cdot (r - F)$$
$$92 = (i \cdot V) / (O \cdot T)$$
$$93 = (g / d) \cdot (o - I)$$
$$94 = (G \cdot p) / (B \cdot l)$$

$$95 = (c - j) \cdot (k - M)$$
$$96 = (D \cdot h) \cdot (K \cdot Q)$$
$$97 = (f \cdot P) / (b - C)$$
$$98 = (J / q) \cdot (N / U)$$
$$99 = (R \cdot S) / (L - m)$$

Answer, page 268

66. HOCKEY LEAGUE

In a league of four hockey teams, each team played the other three. After all six games had been played, the following league table was prepared:

Team	Goals	
	For	Against
A	4	0
B	2	1
C	1	3
D	2	5

Team D drew one game and lost its other two. What was the score in each of the six games?

Answer, page 268

67. NUMBER GRID–I

In how many ways can the numbers from 1 to 9 be arranged in a 3 by 3 array, such that no number has a smaller number than itself appearing either immediately below or immediately to the right of it?

Answer, page 269

68. TRIANGULAREA

ABC is an equilateral triangle. Point P within the triangle is six inches from A, eight inches from B, and ten inches from C. What is the area of the triangle?

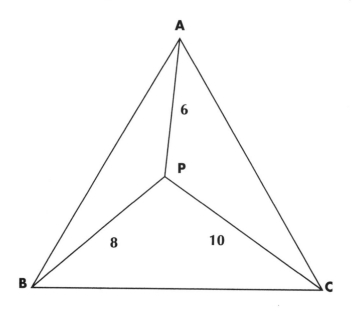

Answer, page 269

69. WORDPLAY–II

The answer to the first of these is "24 hours in a day." Complete the rest.

24 H in a D
5 V in the E A
8 L on a S
1,000 W that a P is W
13 S on the A F
14 L in a S
90 D in a R A
9 L of a C

Answer, page 270

70. MAGIC SQUARE

Find a 4 × 4 magic square that contains 16 different integers, each of which is divisible only by itself and one. As a start, one row has already been completed.

As a further hint, the middle four squares have the same total as the rows, columns, and long diagonals.

53	11	37	1

Answer, page 270

71. BENFORD'S LAW
♦♦♦

Benford's Law applies to the terms of the Fibonacci series, the first few of which are shown below:

1   1   2   3   5   8   13   21   34   . . .

That is, the percentage of numbers in the Fibonacci series beginning with the digit N is log (1 + 1/N) × 100%. Thus, for example, 30.1% (= log (2) × 100%) of the terms in the Fibonacci series begin with a "1." Benford's Law applies to all sorts of other things too, such as share prices, numbers in old magazine articles, and the drainage areas of rivers.

Prove that the percentage of numbers that are predicted to begin with one of the digits between one and nine using the Benford's Law formula total 100%.

Answer, page 270

72. CRYSTAL DROPS

You have several identical crystals that will shatter if dropped from a certain height or above, but which will remain unscathed if dropped from any height lower than this.

You are in a building that has 106 floors. You have already discovered that a crystal dropped from a window on floor 106 will shatter, but you want to know the lowest floor from which you can drop a crystal so that it will shatter.

You could test one floor at a time starting from floor one, but to save time you want a quicker way than this, so long as no more than two more crystals will be shattered during the testing. From which floor should you make the first drop, and what is the maximum number of drops you will require?

Answer, page 271

73. MATHEMATICAL 4'S–II
✦✦✦

Using three 4's, parentheses where necessary, and the eight symbols below as required, find expressions for 119, 268, and 336.

$$+ \quad - \quad \times \quad / \quad . \quad ! \quad \sqrt{} \quad \Sigma$$

The expression Σn denotes the sum of the first n integers, so $\Sigma 4 = 10$. The use of symbols other than those shown, or nonstandard expressions such as $.(\sqrt{4})$ for 0.2, $.(\Sigma 4)$ for 0.1, or $\sqrt{} \sqrt{} \sqrt{} \sqrt{} ... \sqrt{} \sqrt{4}$ for 1, is not permitted.

Answer, page 271

74. ENGLISH CLASS CROSSWORD

In this crossword, clues are of four different types: synonyms, antonyms, anagrams, and a fourth type that must be determined.

1	2		3		4		5	6		7		8		9
10					11	12								
			13											
14							15							
					16									
17								18	19		20			
21		22				23		24					25	
						26								
27				28							29			
								30	31					
32											33			
34								35						

ACROSS

1. Pistol
5. Venomous
10. Pause
11. Coordinate
13. Tear
14. Airs
15. Realize
16. Adze
17. Discern
18. Storm

21. Pleases
24. Dialect
26. Vent
27. Confirm
29. Tail
30. Idol
32. Infidelity
33. Common
34. Patriot
35. Ransom

DOWN

2. Bill
3. Abolish
4. Diet
6. Richest
7. Cater
8. Success
9. Sparing
12. Spoil
16. Young

19. Item
20. Spread
21. Weirdo
22. Bent
23. Sways
24. Urban
25. General
28. Devil
31. Dear

Answer, page 272

75. INSURANCE MANAGERS

A New York insurance company has six account managers, each of whom has a different number of children from none to five. Deduce from the following who has what number of children, the account each manages, and where each lives.

1. Angela has two more children than the manager from Manhattan, who has one more child than the fire manager.

2. The marine manager has two more children than the manager from Queens, who has one more child than Enid.

3. The manager from Staten Island has two more children than Dick, who has one more child than the automotive manager.

4. Chloe has three more children than the property manager.

5. The liability manager has more children than the manager from the Bronx, who is not Enid.

6. The manager from Manhattan, who is not the automotive manager, is not Chloe.

7. Enid is not the property manager, and Fred is not the marine manager.

8. The manager from New Jersey may or may not be Brian.

9. The manager from Brooklyn is not the liability manager, but might be the aviation manager.

Answer, page 272

76. THE EARLY TRAIN

A businessman usually travels home each evening on the same train, and his wife leaves home by car just in time to collect him from the station. One day he caught an earlier train, and having forgotten to tell his wife, he walked to meet the car and was then driven straight home, arriving ten minutes earlier than normal.

The businessman's wife drove at a steady 36 mph each way. Had she been a faster driver, averaging 46 mph, then perhaps surprisingly they would have arrived home just eight minutes earlier rather than ten. This is because being a faster driver and planning to arrive at the station at the same time, the wife would have left home later.

How early was the train?

Answer, page 273

77. LETTERS FOR DIGITS–III

P and Q are five-digit numbers that between them contain all ten digits, as does their product, P × Q. If P = 54,321, what is Q?

Answer, page 273

78. CROSSNUMBERS–II

In this crossnumber puzzle, each number to be entered in the diagram is clued by the number of factors that it has. In this context, both 1 and the number itself are counted as factors. Thus, if 14 were one of the numbers to be entered in the diagram, its clue would be 4, since 14 has four factors (1, 2, 7, and 14).

There is one condition: in the finished diagram, each of the digits from 0 to 9 must appear twice.

Capital letters denote across answers and lowercase letters denote down answers. No answer begins with a zero.

Aa		Bb	c	
C	d		D	e
E		Ff		
G			H	

ACROSS

A.   8
B.   12
C.   2
D.   6
E.   6
F.   24
G.   14
H.   6

DOWN

a.   15
b.   2
c.   9
d.   18
e.   8
f.   10

Answer, page 273

79. GUESS THE THEME–XII

A, B, C, and D each represent a different word or phrase, and they have a common theme. What are the four words or phrases and what is the theme?

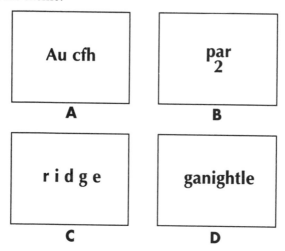

A — **Au cfh**

B — **par 2**

C — **r i d g e**

D — **ganightle**

Answer, page 273

80. FIND THE NUMBER–V

Which two 10-digit numbers, each containing one of each digit, have square roots whose digits are the reverse of one another?

Answer, page 273

81. TIRE WEAR

Tires on Cathy's car last 18,000 miles on the front or 22,000 miles on the back. She has a new set of five tires (including the spare) that she intends to rotate so they can all be replaced at the same time.

A. Assuming no punctures or blowouts, how far can she drive with five tires?

B. Which tires will need to be changed and at what distances if the number of wheel changes she makes is to be kept to a minimum?

Answer, page 273

82. MATCH STARS

The diagram below shows an arrangement of six wooden matches that makes eight triangles.

Without breaking the matches but using lateral thinking, now rearrange the six matches to make eight squares.

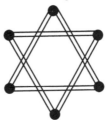

Answer, page 274

83. BOXES

Heather and Lynsey are playing a game of Boxes and have reached the position shown. The object of the game is to complete the most boxes as signified by the initials inside. The rules are that players take turns by adding to the grid a horizontal or vertical line of unit length, and that they have a compulsory extra turn whenever they complete a box. It is Lynsey's turn to play. How can she win?

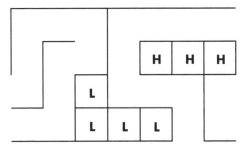

Answer, page 274

84. FIND THE NUMBER–VI

Find a five-digit palindromic number (a number that equals itself when read backward) that has a remainder of 9 when divided by 10, a remainder of 8 when divided by 9, a remainder of 7 when divided by 8, and so on, and whose digits are all odd.

Answer, page 275

85. FARM ACRES

Samos Farm has four straight sides, and its diagonally opposite corners are joined by two straight roads that run north-south and east-west. The lengths of the sides of the farm and the distances between the crossroads and the four corners are all different, and each is an exact number of chains. (An old-fashioned measure of distance that equals 22 yards.)

Given that one side is 35 chains long and that ten square chains make an acre, what is the farm's area measured in acres?

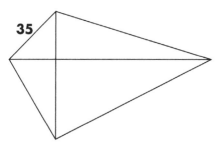

Answer, page 275

86. NUMBER 145
✦✦✦

What property having to do with factorials makes the number 145 interesting?

Answer, page 276

87. GEOMETRY PROOF

Here is a "proof" that all triangles are isosceles. Can you spot the flaw?

Begin with any triangle ABC. Let the bisector of angle A meet the perpendicular bisector of BC at O. The diagrams show O inside and outside the triangle, respectively. Let E and F be the feet of the perpendiculars from O to AB and AC.

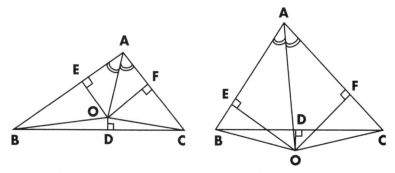

AFO is congruent to AEO, so AE = AF and OE = OF.

BDO is congruent to CDO, so OB = OC.

Thus OEB is congruent to OFC, and EB = FC.

Now, AE = AF and EB = FC, so AE + EB = AF + FC.

Therefore, AB = AC and ABC is isosceles.

Answer, page 276

172   CLASSIC BRAIN TWISTERS

88. GUESS THE THEME–XIII

A, B, C, and D each represent a different word or phrase, and they
have a common theme. What are the four words or phrases and
what is the theme?

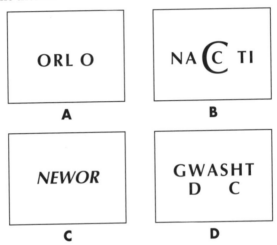

Answer, page 277

89. MATCH ARRANGEMENTS

Arrange six matches in such a way that each one touches four of
the other five.

Answer, page 277

90. WORD CIRCLES–II
✦✦✦

Place three letters in the three empty circles in order that the longest possible word (which may be more than eight letters long) can be spelled out by reading around the circles. You can choose your starting position and whether to read the letters clockwise or counterclockwise.

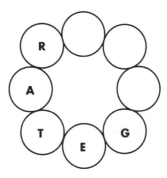

Answer, page 277

91. DISTINGUISHED LETTERS
✦✦✦

In what way are the letters in the top row different from the letters in the bottom row?

C I O Q U
B P R T Y

Answer, page 277

92. CHESS–III

If Black were to play in the position shown, the game would finish immediately, in stalemate. But White is to play, and he can win in just three moves; how?

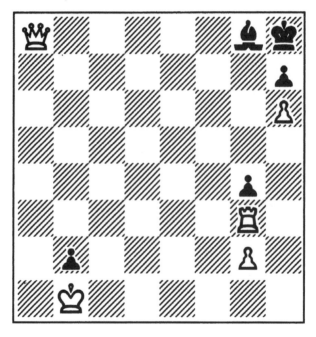

Answer, page 277

93. SYMMETRICAL DOTS

There are six symmetrical ways in which dots can be placed in 16 different squares in an 8 × 8 array such that every row, column, and diagonal (not just the main diagonals from corner to corner) is either empty or has exactly two dots in it. The solution shown below is one such arrangement, and is also symmetrical when divided in half diagonally from top left to bottom right.

Can you find the one solution (ignoring rotations and reflections) that is not symmetrical?

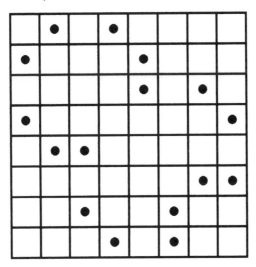

Answer, page 277

94. WORD GRID–II
✦✦✦

Complete the grid using all the letters below so that each row and column containing two or more squares is a word when read from left to right or from top to bottom:

A C C E E E H L N O W

Answer, page 278

95. LYING MEN
✦✦✦

There was a group of three men. When asked a question, one of the men would always answer truthfully, one would always lie, and the third would lie at random. They know who has which habit, but you do not.

How, in only three questions to which the man being asked can only answer "yes" or "no," can you discover which man has which habit? Each of the three questions can be put to one man only, but it need not be to the same man each time. For example, questions one and two could go to the first man, and question three to the second.

Answer, page 278

96. CROSSNUMBERS–III

There are just three clues for this crossnumber:
Every answer is the product of two different primes of equal length.
No answer begins with a zero, and in no answer is a digit repeated.
The digits of the middle six-digit number are in ascending order.

1	2	3	4	5	6
7					
8					
9					
		10			

Answer, page 278

97. PIECE OF CAKE

A rectangular cake is being baked to meet the following requirements:

- The cake can be cut into five rectangular pieces such that each piece has sides that are a whole number of inches long, and
- Sides of the pieces and sides of the original cake all have different measurements.

What is the area of the smallest cake that will meet these requirements?

Answer, page 278

98. GUESS THE THEME XIV

A, B, C, and D each represent a different word or phrase, and they have a common theme. What are the four words or phrases and what is the theme?

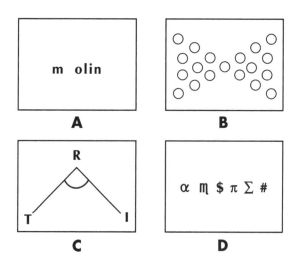

Answer, page 279

99. HIDDEN MESSAGE

Each empty square in this grid is to be filled with a single letter. When read consecutively, the 18 letters spell out a well-known object.

The numbers between the letters provide the only clues. Letting A = 1, B = 2, up to Z = 26, each number indicates the difference between the adjacent letter values. For example, 4 could separate E and A, B and F, and so on. What is the object?

	12		3		14		1		19	
0		13		0		4		14		11
	1		16		10		9		6	
11		19		0		3		14		13
	7		3		13		2		5	

Answer, page 279

100. MAGIC PENTAGON

♦ ♦ ♦

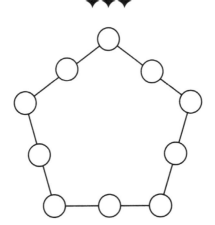

A. Arrange the digits from 0 to 9 in the circles around the pentagon in such a way that the three numbers on each side of the pentagon add up to eleven.

B. Now rearrange the digits in such a way that, starting from a suitable side and moving clockwise, the sums on successive sides are consecutive integers, none of which equals eleven.

Answer, page 279

101. MINCE PIES

There are nine indistinguishable mince pies. Some mincemeat has been removed from one, chosen at random, and put back in another pie, also chosen at random. Thus, either one pie is light and another heavy by the same amount, or else they all have the same weight.

With four trials using a simple balance, either establish that all mince pies have the same weight or identify the light and heavy ones.

Answer, page 279

102. PHRASE GRID–II

What two-word phrase could form the first and fourth rows of the diagram, so that each column contains a five-letter word?

U	V	A	L	O
M	E	S	A	D
Y	T	S	E	L

Answer, page 280

103. BEST IN PRAYERS

If all you knew about Britney Spears was that her name was an anagram of "best in prayers," why might you think her parents were not Catholics? (Hint: look for another anagram, this time one word of thirteen letters.)

Answer, page 280

104. THE DIME

David's mother has three children. She also has three coins from the United States and decides to give one to each child.

Penelope is given a penny.

Nicholas is given a nickel.

What is the name of the child who gets the dime?

Answer, page 280

105. NUMBER 153

The number 153 is interesting for two reasons. The first has something to do with factorials, and the second has to do with cubes. What are these two reasons, and what other three-digit number shares the second property?

Answer, page 280

106. CROSSNUMBERS–IV

In this crossnumber puzzle, none of the numbers to be entered in the diagram begins with a zero.

Aa	b		c	d		e	f
B		g		C	h		
	D						
E				F			
G	i		j	Hk		l	
	I						
J				K			
L							

ACROSS

A. Multiple of j
B. Square
C. 1 – d
D. Fifth power
E. Fourth power
F. Factor of d
G. Square
H. Square
I. Sixth power
J. Multiple of c
K. i – 2b
L. Multiple of E

DOWN

a. c·d
b. Square
c. Square
d. Multiple of F
e. Twice a prime
f. Multiple of j
g. Square
h. Sixth power
i. Prime
j. Cube
k. Square
l. C + d

Answer, page 280

107. GUESS THE THEME–XV

A, B, C, and D each represent a different word or phrase, and they have a common theme. What are the four words or phrases and what is the theme?

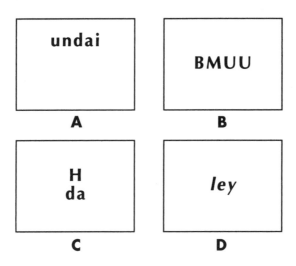

Answer, page 280

108. WHAT DAY IS IT?

Seven friends stranded on a desert island start arguing about what day of the week it is.

Andrew thinks that yesterday was Wednesday.

Dave disagrees, saying that tomorrow is Wednesday.

John maintains that the day after tomorrow is Tuesday.

Pete feels sure that yesterday was not Friday.

Fred believes that today is Tuesday.

Mick says that today is not Sunday, Monday, or Tuesday.

Charlie is adamant that it is Tuesday tomorrow.

If just one of them is right, what day of the week is it?

Answer, page 280

109. DIGIT ARRANGEMENTS

How should the digits from one to eight be arranged as two four-digit numbers so that the product of the two numbers is (**a**) a minimum and (**b**) a maximum?

Answer, page 281

110. CHECKERBOARD SQUARES

Which five of these six pieces can be arranged to form a 5 × 5 checkerboard pattern?

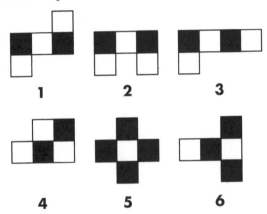

Answer, page 281

111. FASHION EXHIBIT

In a certain fashion show, the exhibits included 36 outfits by Jasper Conran, 35 by Calvin Klein, and 56 by Yves Saint-Laurent. How many outfits did Vivienne Westwood exhibit?

Answer, page 281

112. WORD WHEEL

Place a letter in each of the ten spaces such that:

• Five six-letter words, including one country, are formed by reading in a straight line from each of five letters in the outer ring to the ones at the opposite side, and

• The ten letters in the middle circle, read clockwise, spell out the name of another country.

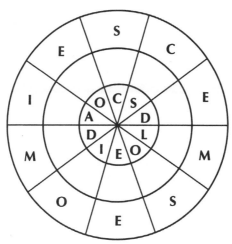

Answer, page 281

113. WEIGHT LOSS

Four women weighed 105, 110, 115, and 120 pounds, respectively. Two weeks ago, Carol announced that she was going on a diet, and the other three immediately decided to join her.

Since starting the diet, no woman's weight has changed by more than five pounds, and all weights are still whole numbers of pounds. Debbie has lost more weight than Miss Easton. Anne weighed ten pounds more than Debbie when they started the diet. Miss Green now weighs ten pounds less than Miss Hope. Miss Frost now weighs seven pounds less than Barbara did before dieting. Miss Hope actually put on weight, but still weighs less than Anne. Barbara has lost more weight than Anne. Miss Easton now weighs four pounds more than Anne.

What are the names and current weights of the four women?

Answer, page 282

114. NUMBER GRID–II

Place the numbers from one to eight in the grid in such a way that each number differs from its neighbors horizontally, vertically, and diagonally by at least two.

Answer, page 282

115. PARALLEL?

The segment below is one-sixth of a circle. Dots A and B on the arc divide that arc into thirds. The other two dots, C and D, are two-thirds of the way from the nearest part of the arc to what would have been the center of the circle.

Are the lines AC and BD parallel? If not, on which side of the segment would they meet if they were extended?

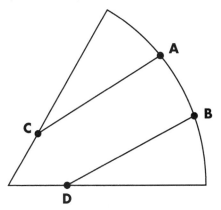

Answer, page 282

116. MISSING NUMBER–II

What number should replace the question mark in the following array?

1	2	3	4	5
1	3	9	21	41
1	4	31	220	1,081
1	5	129	6,949	?

Answer, page 282

117. MAGIC SQUARE–II

In this magic square, A, B, and C are single-digit numbers, 2A means twice A, and so on. Every row, column, and both diagonals add up to the same total. What is that total?

2A	C	2C
A+2B	A+B	A
B	3A	2B

Answer, page 282

118. MAILING LIST

A secretary was asked to organize a mailing to a 10% sample of a company's clients. Rather than just pick 10% of the clients on his mailing list randomly, however, the secretary decided to pick the first client, skip one, pick the next, skip two, pick the next, skip three, pick the next, and so on, until he came to the end of the list. To his surprise, the final client that he picked happened to be the last one on the mailing list. Moreover, as required, he had picked exactly 10% of the total.

How many names were on the mailing list?

Answer, page 282

119. RECTANGLE FORMATION

The piece below on the left comprises three squares of unit length. What is the smallest rectangle that can be covered with pieces of this shape in a way such that no two pieces form a 2 × 3 rectangle (as shown below on the right)?

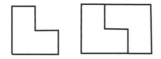

Answer, page 283

120. CHESS–IV
✦✦✦

On a regular 8 × 8 chessboard, shown below, only five queens are needed in order to ensure that all unoccupied squares are attacked.

How many queens are needed on an 11 × 11 board?

Answer, page 283

121. PRICE CHECK
✦✦✦

Emma buys seven items. The prices of the items are all different, and the total cost is $10.71. Emma checks this on her calculator, but inadvertently multiplies the amounts together instead of adding. The result, with correct treatment of decimal points, is also $10.71. What are the prices of the seven items?

Answer, page 283

122. RUBBER RING

The diagram below shows five flat interlocked rings lying on the ground. Four are made of a rigid metal; the fifth is made of rubber. Which is the rubber one?

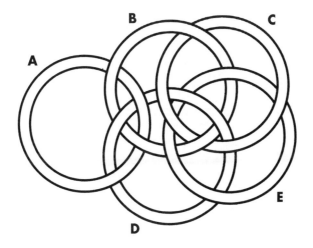

Answer, page 284

123. SWITCHING TRACKS

The diagram below shows two railway lines with a crossover track. The task for the two engine drivers is to exchange the two wagons on the top track with the two on the bottom track, with the wagons finishing in the same order from left to right as they started. What makes the task difficult is that the usable stretch of straight track at the bottom right will take only two wagons, while the usable stretch at the top right will take only two wagons and an engine. How can the drivers accomplish the task?

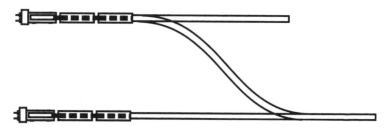

Answer, page 284

ANSWERS

MIND TEASER
ANSWERS

THE HARD WAY

P A S S E R
P A S S E R
P A S S R E
P A S R S E
P S A R S E
S P A R S E

The key is that the first (or second) move must be to switch the two S's. That's because the indicated permutation is an even permutation that must be accomplished in an odd number of moves.

WHO'S NEXT?

17, 19, 23, 29, **31**   OR   17, 19, 23, 29, **37**

In the first case, the listing is just a partial listing of prime numbers, and 31 is the next on the list. In the second case, the gap between each successive member of the sequence is growing (2, 4, 6) so the next member must be 29 + 8, or 37.

CODE DEPENDENCE

If you write 3 1 2 1 2 5 as 3 1 2 12 5, you get CABLE. If you write it as 3 12 1 25, you get CLAY!

WET AND WILD

The cat's hunting instinct had been activated, and sorely tested, by nearby activity, so it attacked the bird—momentarily interrupting a badminton game.

TWO FOR ONE

Blue   MOROSE, INDIGO
Rank   GROSS, MAJOR
Frank   HOT DOG, CANDID
Ground ___ BALL, BEEF

TAKING NOTES

Face the music.

BRICK BY BRICK

A total of 30 bricks would be needed to make the chimney; five rows of six apiece.   Note that the aerial view of the chimney looks like this:

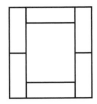

ENDLESS SUMMER

14,850. Begin with the verse "99 bottles of beer on the wall, 99 bottles of beer, take 1 down, pass it around, 98 bottles of beer on the wall." The numbers of the song can be displayed as shown at the right.

The sum of the third column is 99. If that 99 is placed atop the fourth column, we see that the total sum is three times the

99	99	1	98
98	98	1	97
97	97	1	96
		. . . .	
3	3	1	2
2	2	1	1
1	1	1	0

sum of the positive integers from 1 through 99. But that sum equals $(99 \times 100)/2$, so the total sum equals $99 \times 150 = 14,850$.

FIVE OF A KIND

A. $(333/3)/3 = 37$
B. $4! + 4! + (4! + 4)/4 = 55$

HALF A SHAKE

Not five! The earthquake with the higher reading is more powerful by a factor of the square root of 10, or just under 3.2.

IN THE MIDDLE

milliliter; lighthouse (also eighth, lighthearted, ichthyosaur, diphthong, knighthood), piquant (also antiquated, reliquary); and jawbone (also drawback, jawbreaker, sawbuck, lawbreaker).

SURE THING

At the same time as she bought the mower, she simply also picked up a new combination lock. She placed it on the shed for the week and, on Christmas Eve, she put the original lock back into place.

CLOSE QUARTERS

Six. When you place three quarters in the manner shown below (the gray circle is the quarter in the middle), the centers of the three quarters form the vertices of an equilateral triangle. Each angle of this triangle must be 60 degrees, so the complete 360-degree circle will accommodate six such triangles.

BASE TEN

The sum of the numbers in the tenth row would be 1,000. Observe that the sums of rows 1, 2, and 3 are 1, 8, and 27 respectively. In each case, the sum equals the cube of the row number, and that pattern continues. The sum of the tenth row therefore equals 10 cubed, or 1,000.

SEEING STARS

Each of the actors and actresses starred in a TV show that was also the name of a song. The group or musical performer who did that song is given here in parenthesis.

Julia: Diahann Carroll • (The Beatles)
Jeopardy: Alex Trebek • (The Greg Kihn Band)
Taxi: Danny Devito • (Harry Chapin)
Good Times: Jimmy Walker • (Chic)
Angie: Donna Pescow • (The Rolling Stones)

FENDER BENDER

The accident could be explained by a layout such as the one below, in which Redington Road forms a loop that comes back to meet Warren Street:

DOUBLE CROSS–I

S	T	A	T	E
T				A
I	Solution 1			R
F				L
F	A	I	R	Y

R	I	V	E	R
I				E
G	Solution 2			L
I				A
D	E	C	A	Y

ICE FOLLIES

Skater E is the winner.

To see why, note that skaters B and D would have received one and two points, respectively, for the short program, while A, C, and E would have received 0.5, 1.5, and 2.5 points, respectively. Because the score for the long program is a whole number, the only possible three-way tie would be between skaters A, C, and E. But the only way for that to happen would be for skater E to win the long program; in that case, according to the tie-breaking rules, she would win the entire competition.

HIDDEN PATTERN

If you start with the first letter of each word and count every other letter, the result is also a word:

R e **A** l **I** g **N**
S h **A** l **L** o **T**
C h **A** r **R** e **D**
I n **D** u **L** g **E**

SIGN OF THE TIMES

$26 \times 1.04 = 26 + 1.04 = 27.04$. In general, any pair of numbers of the form X, X/(X-1) has the property that the sum equals the product: (3, 3/2), (4, 4/3), and so on. The solution to this problem is 26, 26/25.

ODD MAN OUT

All four men also have numbers hidden in their names, either forward or backward. In Steve Allen's case, there are two—but the letters aren't together.

Jay L<u>ENO</u>
Vladimir L<u>ENIN</u>
Len D<u>EIGHT</u>on
(S)<u>T</u>(<u>E</u>ve) Alle(<u>N</u>)

CHECKERBOARD SQUARE

68 circles will fit, as long as you alternate the columns.

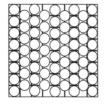

TIME WARP

A section of Western Florida (including Pensacola) is in the Central Time Zone. A section of Oregon (including Ontario, OR) is in the Mountain Time Zone, only one hour apart. Those two areas will have the same time for one hour at the end of daylight savings time, because clocks "fall back" at 2:00 a.m. one Sunday morning, and that time moves from east to west. So, for the hour until the end of daylight savings time in the Mountain Time Zone, Pensacola, FL, and Ontario, OR, will show the same time.

SPEED DIALING

One scenario is that the wife had been calling from upstairs, then went downstairs to get the phone number of the restaurant. She then called the restaurant from the kitchen phone, later calling her husband from the upstairs (i.e., bedroom) phone. The point is that the redial button is specific to the actual handset, and doesn't apply to the entire line.

A PERFECT STRANGER

She was carrying a letter and was on her way to the closest mailbox. The man in question was a postman.

A SECOND KIND OF CUT

The diagram at left creates two pieces of the same shape, as long as the vertical lines at the left and right of the smaller piece are made at points two-thirds of the way along their respective squares. (This dissection is the creation of Michael Reid. It's a beauty!)

ATTENTION SPORTS FANS

1 2 3 4 5 6 7 8 9 10
0 1 1 1 1 3 2 4 4 5

The numbers in the nth column of the second row give the number of distinct ways of scoring n points in football. Here is the complete list:

Points / Method

- 1 / Impossible
- 2 / Safety
- 3 / Field goal
- 4 / Two safeties
- 5 / Field goal and safety
- 6 / Two field goals; three safeties; one touchdown
- 7 / A field goal and two safeties; a touchdown with extra point
- 8 / Four safeties; two field goals and a safety; a touchdown and a safety; a touchdown plus two-point conversion
- 9 / Three field goals; a touchdown and a field goal; a touchdown with extra point and a safety; a field goal and three safeties.
- 10 / A touchdown with an extra point and a field goal; five safeties; two safeties and two field goals; a touchdown and two safeties; a touchdown with a two-point conversion and a safety.

SHOW TIME

STAYING THE SAME

$$\sqrt{10} - 3 = \sqrt{\frac{1}{10} + 3}$$

WORD CHAIN

KEY	HORSE
CHAIN	FLY
LETTER	BALL
PERFECT	POINT
PITCH	BLANK
DARK	CHECK
HORSE	OFF
	KEY

HAPPY ANNIVERSARY

The 35th season of the camp took place in 1999, not 2000, so it definitely took place in the 20th century, whether you consider the 21st century to have begun on January 1, 2000 or January 1, 2001.

SHORT BUT SWEET

25 pitches would be enough, in theory—and only on the assumption that the pitcher was pitching for the away team! The way this could happen is if every batter swung at the first pitch, with 24 out of 25 hitting into an out and the other one hitting a home run. Assuming that the pitcher's team never scored at all, the final score would be 1–0 in favor of the home team, which then wouldn't have to bat in the last half of the ninth inning. (Thanks to "Test your Baseball Literacy," by R. Wayne Schmittberger, for suggesting this little gem.)

PICKING UP STICKS

A. For the first problem, there are 10 ways of choosing the three sticks (five choices for the first, four for the second, and three for the third, but you have to divide by six—the number of ways of rearranging the three chosen sticks—because a choice of, say, 2–4–5 yields the same triangle as a choice of 5–2–4). Of those ten ways of choosing three sticks, only three result in triangles: 2–3–4, 2–4–5, and 3–4–5. That's because the sum of any two sides must be greater than the third side.

B. For the second problem, there are 1,140 ways of choosing the three sticks: $(20 \times 19 \times 18)/6$. But only these six combinations satisfy the Pythagorean Theorem: 3–4–5, 6–8–10, 9–12–15, 12–16–20, 5–12–13, and 8–15–17. The chance of creating a right triangle is therefore $6/1{,}140 = 1/190$.

ALL WET

As long as you maintain a high enough speed, a wind foil will form across the top of the sunroof opening, keeping the passengers dry. But the foil doesn't operate at low rates of speed; when the second driver slowed down, the rain came pouring in.

SPACE SAVERS

Each of the eight three-letter words is an abbreviation for a U.S. airport:

FAT   Fresno
OAK   Oakland
LAX   Los Angeles
SAT   San Antonio
DEN   Denver
SEA   Seattle
PIT   Pittsburgh
LIT   Little Rock

ROMAN CROSSWORD

	M	C	L	V		M	M	M
M	M	I	I	I		D	I	M
C	L	V	I		M	C	M	X
X	X	I		L	X		I	V
		L	I	V	I	D		
M	D		I	I		C	M	V
M	I	D	I		M	C	M	I
C	L	I		C	I	V	I	C
C	L	X		L	X	I	X	

THE MAX FACTOR

There were 11 rows. The conditions of the problem suggest that 319 is a composite number, and in fact $319 = 11 \times 29$. Eleven rows of 29 people would be much more likely than 29 rows of 11 people!

ON THE LINE

The probability that the player will make only one free throw is slightly more than 4/25. If he makes his first one (probability 4/5) and misses his second one (probability 1/5), we get a compound probability of $(4/5)(1/5) = 4/25$. But if he missed the first free throw, he will try to miss the second one so that he or a teammate can put in the rebound. (There is no sense in making the second free throw, because the opponents would then have the ball with a one-point lead and only 1.7 seconds on the clock. The reason that the final probability is slightly more than 4/25 is that the player, in deliberately trying to miss his second free throw, might screw up and put it in the basket!

BINARY OPERATION

For a number to be divisible by 15 it must be divisible by both 3 and 5. A number is divisible by 3 if and only if the sum of its digits is divisible by 3, so the number in question, consisting of only 0's and 1's, must have three 1's in it. Add a zero and we get our answer: 1,110.

QUIT WHILE YOU'RE AHEAD

The probability that the first player will lose the game equals 6/11. To see why, note that there is a 1/6 chance that he will lose on his first shot. On the other hand, there is a 25/36 probability that he will get to shoot again, because that is the probability that both he and his opponent will miss their first shots. At that point, the game essentially starts over again. Putting all of this into an equation, we get P = 1/6 + (25/36)P, so (11/36)P = 1/6 and P = 6/11.

GETTING SHEEPISH

The area that the sheep have to themselves is precisely one acre. To account for this surprising result, check out the diagram. The big circle indicates the area available to the dog. (Note that the big circle must intersect with the third vertex of the triangle because it is a right triangle.) By using the Pythagorean Theorem and the formula $A = pr^2$ for a circle, we see that the area of the two smaller semicircles must equal the area of the larger semicircle, so A + C + B + D = F. But F = C + E + D, so we have A + C + B + D = C + E + D and therefore A + B = E. We know that E equals one acre, and A + B is the area that the sheep have to themselves, so that does it.

DOUBLE CROSS–II

S	A	L	A	D
P				R
E		Solution 1		A
R				I
M	A	S	O	N

R	O	M	A	N
I				A
G		Solution 2		D
H				I
T	I	L	E	R

CIRCULAR REASONING

The probability is 3/4. To see why, first position a point at the bottom of a circle. Then imagine a second point starting at the bottom and traveling clockwise around the circumference. With the second point at the starting point, the third point could be placed anywhere on the circle and the three points would have to be in a common semicircle. As the second point starts its clockwise journey, the options for the third point would shrink somewhat; specifically, if x denotes the number of degrees traveled by the second point, then the third point could be placed anywhere within an arc of $360 - x$ degrees to ensure that the three points would all fit in a semicircle. This pattern would continue until the second point was at the very top of the circle (when, technically, the third point could again be placed anywhere), and then the pattern would reverse itself as the second point traveled down the right side of the circle. For any value between 0 and 360 (for the second point), the lined area of the diagram to the right indicates the possibilities for the second point to satisfy the semicircle condition. You will note that the lined area is precisely $3/4$ the size of the square. That does it!

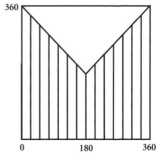

NORSE CODE

The answer is Eric, as in Eric *the Red*. Note that each of the nonsense combinations makes sense when attached to ___thered:

gathered, **sli**thered, **smo**thered, **wi**thered, **bo**thered, **la**thered, **fea**thered

BACK AND FORTH

The original number was 13. Squaring it gives 169. Reverse that to get 961, and take the square root to get 31. Another reversal gets you back from where you started.

BUMPER CROP

From lightest to heaviest, the watermelons weigh 9, 11, 13, 14, and 17 pounds.

One place to begin the solution is by noting that the weights of the two heaviest watermelons add up to 31, so one must be even and one must be odd.

On the other hand, the two lightest add up to 20, so either both are even or both are odd. Which is it? Well, altogether there are six even combinations (20, 22, 24, 26, 28, and 30) and four odd combinations (23, 25, 27, and 31). If the lightest two were both even, then the five watermelons would be E, E, ?, O, E or E, E, ?, E, O. In either case, you would get at least six odd combinations, because the one O added to any of the E's would yield an odd sum. So the lightest two watermelons must both have odd weights, and given that they add up to 20, the combination {9, 11} is a good place to start. From there you need a 13, 14, and 17, and the list is complete.

You can check that those five weights, when combined in pairs, do indeed yield the set {20, 22, 23, 24, 25, 26, 27, 28, 30, 31}.

TWO GUYS

Skipjack
Stephanotis
Herbal
Ricochet
Calgary

SQUARE DEAL

The answer is 70. To count the number of sub-squares on a 24 by 24 chessboard, it helps to look first at a 3 by 3 case.

In a 3 by 3 chessboard, there are 9 squares of size 1 by 1, 4 squares of size 2 by 2 (each of the 4 squares in the 2 by 2 square at the bottom left could itself be the bottom left square for a 2 by 2 sub-square!), and, of course, 1 square of size 3 by 3, for a total of 13. In general, the number of sub-squares on an n by n chessboard equals the sum of all squares less than or equal to n, which is given by the formula $n(n + 1)(2n + 1)/6$.

For $n = 24$, the number of sub-squares equals $24(25)(49)/6$, or 4,900. This is 70^2, so the side of the big chessboard must be 70 squares long.

DON'T FEEL STUMPED

By drawing additional lines, we divide the equilateral triangle into six congruent right triangles. Because these triangles are all "30-60-90" triangles (the measures of the three angles), in each case the shorter side is equal to one-half the hypotenuse. But we also know that these triangles meet at the center of the circle, so the "stump" of the tree must equal half the radius, or one-fourth the total height of the tree.

NOT-SO-TRUE CRIME

The crime was committed near the slopes of a mountain. The victim was snowshoeing alongside the mountain when the perpetrator fired his shotgun, starting a fatal avalanche.

OUT OF SIGHT

ryaN O'NEal
oMAR SHarif
juLIE Nixon eisenhower

THE DATING GAME

1953, 1958, and 1959. Note that 53 and 59 are prime numbers, and no prime years after 1931 have the desired property (January 31, 1931 = 1/31/31).

Although 58 is not prime, its prime factorization is 2×29, and 2/29/58 does not work because 1958 was not a leap year: There was no February 29, 1958!

WHAT'S IN A NAME?

Two presidents: Harrison Ford
Two New York City mayors: Lindsay Wagner
Two cowboy portrayers: Wayne Rogers

ROADS SCHOLARSHIP

A reckless driver had caused an accident on a TULANE highway. Unfortunately for him, he was booked by the nastiest COPPIN STATE police history. The driver tried to make excuses: "With all that fog, I couldn't SIENA thing out there, and the rain made me SKIDMORE." At that point the man in blue responded angrily, "Look, mister, either you make BAYLOR spend the night in jail."

MORE FUN WITH DATES

The date in question is October 24th, 2026, or 10/24/26.

OPEN AND SHUT CASE

The problem was that the toilet paper holder blocked the drawer—at least when the roll was mostly full. By the time the roll had wound down a good part of the way, it no longer blocked the drawer.

THE BLACK HOLE

The black hole didn't go anywhere: The illusion is caused by the fact that the two big "triangles" are not in fact the same shape.

Note, in the drawings below, that the slope of the top triangle in the left diagram is 3/5, whereas the slope of the other triangle in that diagram is 5/8. The slight difference (0.6 versus 0.625) is barely noticeable to the eye, but it means that the whole "triangle"…

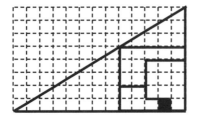 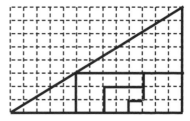

…actually bulges slightly.

SWEET SIXTEEN

The left diagram below shows one arrangement where the columns all have equal sums. The way to produce this solution is to first create the diagram on the right, in which the digits 1 2, 3, 4 have been staggered both horizontally and vertically. Clearly the columns of this diagram have equal sums, and the left-hand diagram is obtained by adding 0, 4, 8, and 12 to rows one, two, three, and four, respectively, and these operations keep the column sums equal.

1	2	3	4
8	5	6	7
11	12	9	10
14	15	16	13

1	2	3	4
4	1	2	3
3	4	1	2
2	3	4	1

NO RULER REQUIRED

Line B is the longest, A is in the middle, and C is the shortest. To see why B is longer than A, we draw a couple of extra lines, as seen here, showing that the line in B exceeds the radius of the circle. But the line in C is shorter than the radius of the circle, so A is in the middle.

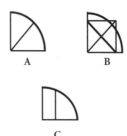

A

B

C

TOUGH NEIGHBORHOOD

Here is one solution:

	7	
3	1	4
5	8	6
	2	

WHAT NOW?

3. The ten words contain the initials of the first ten presidents, as follows:

George Washington • (GoWn)
John Adams • (JAb)
Thomas Jefferson • (TraJectory)
James Madison • (JaM)
James Monroe • (JuMp)
John Quincy Adams • (JacQuArd)
Andrew Jackson • (AJar)
Martin Van Buren • (MoVaBle)
William Henry Harrison • (WHicH)
John Tyler • (JeT)

The initials of the eleventh president, James Knox Polk, are found in JacKPot.

CUTTING CORNERS

50. By drawing a few lines, we see that the radius must be the hypotenuse of a right triangle, as at the right. Note that the three sides of the right triangle form an arithmetic progression with a difference of d between consecutive pairs. The only triangle that satisfies this condition is the triangle (3d, 4d, 5d), so the radius is 5d. Each side of the square is therefore 10d, so 50 of the little rectangles fit in the square.

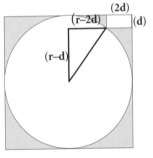

TOUGH TWISTERS
ANSWERS

TWINS

I spoke to Peter. If a person always lies or alternately, always tells the truth, he cannot admit that he is lying (if this person were a liar, he would be telling the truth, and if this person were honest, he would be lying). Therefore, Paul could not have answered my question. Peter could answer about Paul without contradicting himself. What we don't know is who the liar is.

TWIN STATISTICS

More than 3% of the population are twins. Out of 100 births, 97 are single and 3 are twins. That's 103 babies in total, six of which are twins, which represents 5.8% of the population.

PLACE YOUR CARDS

From left to right: queen of spades, six of diamonds, and ace of hearts.

THE PROFESSOR AND HIS FRIEND

Professor Zizoloziz wins. Every player takes an odd number of matches per play. After the first player goes, there will always be an odd number of matches left. After the second player goes, there will always be an even number of matches left. Therefore, the second player is the winner.

IRREGULAR CIRCUIT

300 yards from point A. The first passing point can be considered as a new starting point. Therefore, the new passing point will be 150 yards away.

ECONOMICAL PROGRESSION

1, 6, 11, 16, 21, 26. Other solutions are also possible.

SKIN AND SHOES

It is enough to look at only one shoe. If, for example, the white man's right shoe is red, the left one has to be black. This means that the black man will have one left red shoe and one right white shoe, and so on.

EVE'S ENIGMA

Thursday. The snake is lying, because it says that today is Saturday and tomorrow is Wednesday. Therefore, today is one of the days when the snake lies (Tuesday, Thursday, and Saturday). It cannot be Saturday or else the snake would not be lying in one statement. Nor can it be Tuesday, for the same reason. It can only be Thursday.

WHAT MONTH—I

February of a leap year. If a month starts and ends with the same day of the week, it must have a complete number of weeks plus one more day. The only possible month is a 29-day February.

WHAT MONTH—II

August. In order to add up to 38, it can only be the highest possible number for the last Monday of a month (31) and the highest for the first Thursday of a month (7). Therefore, both last month and the current must have 31 days. The only two 31-day months in a row in the same calendar year are July and August.

UP AND DOWN

22 steps. While Zizoloziz goes up the entire staircase, I descend the staircase except for 11 steps (7 at the top + 4 at the bottom). Since he goes twice as fast as me, the entire staircase is 2×11 steps.

BROKEN M

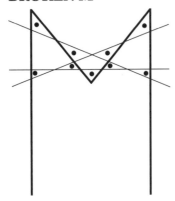

SOCCER SCORES—I

The Eagles had 5 points. There were 10 matches in the tournament with a total of 20 points to be won by the teams. The table already has 15 points assigned. Therefore, the remaining 5 points must belong to the Eagles.

SOCCER SCORES—II

Lions 0, Tigers 0. Lions 1, Bears 0. Tigers 1, Bears 1. The Lions could only win 3 points by winning one match and tying another. Since they only scored one goal, the results must be 1-0 and 0-0. The Bears tied one and lost the other match. The scores must have been 1-1 and 0-1. Their tied game must have been against the Tigers. So the Lions beat the Bears 1-0, and the Lions tied the Tigers 0-0.

PROHIBITED CONNECTION

Each middle digit (2, 3, 4, and 5) can only be connected to three others (for example, 2 can only be connected to 4, 5, and 6). There are two circles with four connections. We can only put 1 and 6 in them. Once you insert these, the rest is easy to figure out. Another solution exists where the order of the numbers is switched, so 1 and 6 switch, as do 2 and 5, and 3 and 4.

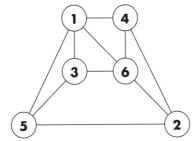

WHAT TIME IS IT—I

5:00. From here, the minute hand will take 30 minutes to reach 6, and the hour hand will take an entire hour.

WHAT TIME IS IT—II

There are two possible times in this situation: 5:15 (the minute hand takes 15 minutes to reach 6 and the hour hand takes 45) and 3:45 (the minute hand takes 45 minutes to reach 6 and the hour hand takes 2 hours and 15 minutes, which is 135 minutes).

WHAT TIME IS IT—III

2:12. The hour hand is at the first minute mark after 2, and the minute hand is on the next minute mark.

WHAT TIME IS IT—IV

9:48. The minute hand is on 48 minutes and the hour hand is on the next minute mark.

CONCENTRIC

30 square inches. We turn the small square as shown in the picture at the right. We can see that it is half the size of the big one, as indicated by the dotted lines. These dotted lines divide the large square into 8 triangles, and the small square into 4 triangles.

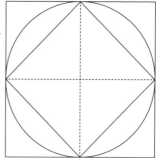

JOHN CASH

The reward was 125 dollars. If you erase 1, you have 25 left, which is one fifth the original amount. If you erase 2, you have 5 left, which is one fifth of this amount.

To get 125, find a two-digit number in which you can take the first digit off and the result is one fifth of the number. The only possible number is 25; $25 \times 5 = 125$.

NEW RACE

One car goes twice as fast as the other. The first crossing took place at point A. Consider A as a new starting point. Do the same for every crossing point. Since they drove at consistent speeds, the distances from A to B, B to C, and C to A are the same. After point A, one car must have driven twice the distance as the other to reach B at the same time. Therefore, one goes twice as fast as the other.

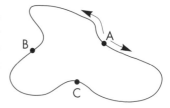

RUSSIAN ROULETTE

The arsenic is in the jar labeled "SUGAR." We know that the snuff is above the salt. They cannot be on the right side, because then the salt would be in the jar labeled "SALT." They cannot be in the center either, because then the second answer would not be true since the coffee and sugar would not be next to each other. Therefore, they are on the left. So the coffee and sugar are in the jars marked "TEA" and "SALT," respectively, leaving arsenic for either the jar marked "ARSENIC" or "SUGAR." Since it's not in the correctly labeled jar, it must be in the jar marked "SUGAR," and the tea is in the jar marked "ARSENIC."

THE CALCULATOR KEYS

There are two possibilities:
1. Change the 4 with the 5 and the 2 with the 8.
   $729 - 546 = 183$.
2. Change the 3 with the 9 and the 4 with the 6.
   $783 - 654 = 129$.

NICE DISCOUNTS

You first buy books for $80 and, the next day, for $70, which represents a discount of $70 \times .08 = \$5.60$. (It will be the same result by inverting the order of the purchases, first the $70 purchase and the next day the $80 one.)

HOROSCOPE

The teacher is a Pisces. This conversation could have only taken place on February 29. She was 29 then. Six days later (March 6), having turned 30, it becomes true that the date is one fifth of her age. This means her birthday occurs during the six first days of March.

ENIGMATIC FARES

98999 and 99000. The tickets are consecutive in number. If the professor had answered "yes" to the question about the five digits of one ticket adding up to 35, the friend could have not figured out the numbers. There would have been several possibilities (78659 and 78660, 36989 and 36990, etc.), so the professor must have answered that indeed none of the tickets added up to 35.

The digits on both tickets add up to 62 (an even number), which means that the first one must end in a 9. If it ended in only one 9, one ticket would add up to 35. Let's call the first ticket ABCD9 and the second one ABC(D + 1)0. The sum is $A + B + C + D + 9 + A + B + C + D + 1 = 62$, meaning that $A + B + C + D + 9 = 35$. If it ended in two 9s, the sum of both tickets would give us an odd number.

Therefore, the ticket must end in three 9s and no more than three, or the sum wouldn't be 62. We can call the tickets AB999 and A(B+1)000, where B is not 9. The sum of both is $2 \times (A + B) + 28 = 62$.
Therefore, $A = 9$ and $B = 8$.

MONTE CARLO

He lost. Every time that Hystrix wins, his money increases 1.5 times (with $100, he bets $50 and if he wins, he has $150). When he loses, his money is reduced by half. So a win-loss combination results in a loss of one quarter of his money. The more he plays, the more money he loses, even though he wins the same number of times as he loses.

STRANGERS IN THE NIGHT

The blonde woman killed Mr. Farnanski. There are only four true statements. Only one person is guilty. Therefore, three of the "I'm innocent" statements are true. Only one more statement can be true, and this must be the one made by the man in the dark suit or by the blonde woman.

Therefore, "The brunette killed him" and "One of the men killed him" are false statements, so the blonde woman is the killer.

THE FOREIGNERS AND THE MENU

They could have ordered ABCDD their first night (finding out what D is), AEFGG the second night (finding out what G is and what A is, since they had ordered it the previous night, too), and BEHII the third night, (finding out what I, B, and E are). This leaves C, F, and H out, and since they had never ordered these dishes twice and each came on a different night, they should know what they are.

FORT KNOX JUMPING FROGS—I

Move 5 onto 2, 3 onto 7, 1 onto 4, and 6 onto 8.

FORT KNOX JUMPING FROGS—II

Move 5 onto 2, 3 onto 7,
4 onto 13, 6 onto 1,
12 onto 9, 11 onto 14,
and 10 onto 8.

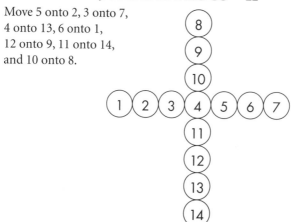

FORT KNOX JUMPING FROGS—III

Move 5 onto 12, 6 onto 4,
10 onto 11, 8 onto 1,
3 onto 2, and 9 onto 7.

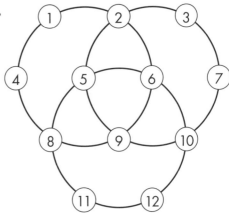

FORT KNOX JUMPING FROGS—IV

Move 16 onto 3, 8 onto 5, 17 onto 11,
10 onto 18, 2 onto 15, 7 onto 1, 13 onto 9,
14 onto 20, 12 onto 19, and 6 onto 4.

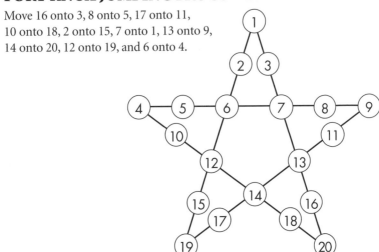

FORT KNOX JUMPING FROGS—V

Move 1 onto 4, 10 onto 7, 11 onto 14,
20 onto 17, 5 onto 3, 6 onto 8, 15 onto 13,
16 onto 18, 2 onto 12, and 19 onto 9.

THE HAREM

There were seven locks. Let's name the locks A, B, C, D, E, F, and G. The vizier had keys for A, B, C, D, E, and F. One of the slaves had the keys for A, B, C, and G. Another one, for A, D, E, and G. Another, for B, D, F, and G. And the last, for C, E, F, and G. With seven locks, Tamerlane's system works—but not with fewer locks.

THE DIVIDING END

The number is 381654729.

If the number is ABCDEFGHI, B, D, F, and H are even numbers. The rest are odd numbers. ABCDE can be divided evenly by 5, thus E = 5.

ABCD can be divided evenly by 4. Therefore, CD can also be divided evenly by 4, and since C is an odd number, D can only be 2 or 6.

ABCDEF can be divided evenly by 6 (by 2 and by 3). Since ABC can be divided by 3, DEF can be also. Consequently, DEF is 258 or 654.

You can deduce the rest from here.

THE ISLAND AND THE ENGLISHMEN

Six Englishmen. Let's draw four circles representing the clubs. Every two clubs have one member in common, so we draw a line from each circle to one point (an Englishman). Each dot is connected to two lines. This is the situation in the illustration, indicating six Englishmen.

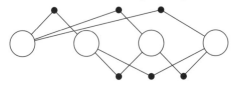

LOGIC APPLES

Alonso 1, Bertrand 2, George 3, and Kurt 5.

Alonso could not have eaten 5 or more. Bertrand could not have eaten only one or he would have known that he hadn't eaten more than Alonso. Neither could he have eaten 5 or more. He could have eaten 2, 3, or 4. George figures this out, although he still doesn't know if he ate more than Bertrand. This means that George must have eaten 3 or 4. Kurt can only deduce the other amounts if he ate 5. And the rest, in order to add up to 11, must have eaten 1, 2, and 3.

ADDED CORNERS

The 8 cannot be in a corner, so we have to put it in a square. The 7 must go in a square, too. This makes it easy to figure out the rest.

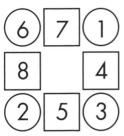

RECTANGLES

Both rectangles have the same area, 40 square inches. If you draw the dotted line you will see that the line divides the inclined figure into two equal pairs of triangles on both sides.

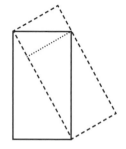

A WARM FAREWELL

10 men and 6 women. The number of handshakes and kisses adds up to 55. Each Porter said good-bye to each Robinson. If we multiply the number of members of both families, the result should be 55. There are two possibilities: $55 = 11 \times 5$ (one family with 11 members and other one with 5), or $55 = 55 \times 1$ (which could not be possible, since a family is not formed by only one person).

We now analyze the handshakes following the same procedure. There are two possibilities: $21 = 7 \times 3$ (7 men in one family and 3 in the other) or $21 = 21 \times 1$ (which could not be possible, because none of these families has so many members, as seen above). Therefore, one family is formed by 7 men and 4 women, and the other by 3 men and 2 women.

TOUCHING SQUARES

14 squares.

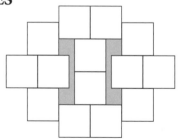

FOUR MINUS ONE IS A CRIME

The killer is Mr. A. To go from A to B you will always travel an even number of blocks. However, in the statements there is an odd number (13 blocks from A to the corner of the meeting and from there to B's house). So, either A or B is lying. A similar condition applies to A and C. You will need an odd number of blocks, but the statements talk about an even number. So, either A or C is lying. Therefore, A is lying.

ON THE ROUTE OF MARCO POLO

The road signs each point to a different village. The sum of distances in one direction and the sum in the opposite direction must be equal. This can only be achieved with $10 + 7 = 8 + 5 + 4$. Therefore, the signs with 10 and 7 point in one direction and the three others point in the opposite direction.

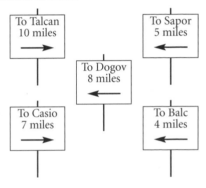

ON THE ROAD

10 miles from Philadelphia.

The five signs indicate the following distances: 98, 76, 54, 32, 10.

Other possible sequences include: 90, 81, 72, 63, 54 and 90, 72, 54, 36, 18. However, in all cases the distance from the final sign to Philadelphia is greater.

EQUAL VISION

Six watchmen. One way to do it is shown below.

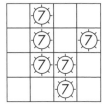

BLOOD AND SAND

Lincoln Dustin died at 5:30. At first the commissioner thought that Mr. Dustin had inverted the hourglass at 7:30 (which would account for the 15 hours that the hourglass took to finish). The evident suspect is Begonias, who was at the mansion at the time. Then Begonias told him that he had inverted the hourglass. This made the commissioner think that Mr. Dustin had inverted the hourglass and then Begonias did as well, which means that the time between both inversions counted twice toward the total amount of time. Since the total time was 3 hours, Begonias inverted the hourglass one and a half hours after Mr. Dustin had. If Begonias said that he had inverted it at 7 P.M., this means that Mr. Dustin inverted it at 5:30.

INTERNATIONAL SUMMIT

A-Spanish, French, Portuguese; B-all; C-all except French; D-Spanish; and E-French and Italian.

Draw a table with five rows and five columns, making the languages the column headers and the people the row headers. Statement 1 tells us that B and C speak English. Mark an X in the corresponding cells. Statement 1 also tells us that D does not speak English. Mark a zero in the corresponding cell. In addition, statement 1 tells us B, C, and D speak Spanish. Mark it in the table. Follow the same procedure for statement 2 and statement 3. Statement 3 explains that the only common language to C and E is Italian, and since C also speaks English and Spanish, we can write zeroes for E in those columns. In a similar way, write a zero for French in C.

This is how the table will look at this point:

	Eng.	Sp.	Fr.	Port.	Ital.
A			X		
B	X	X	X		
C	X	X	O		X
D	O	X			
E	O	O	X		X

We can see that three people speak Spanish and French. Add another X for Spanish, since it is the most common language.

From statement 6 we need one person who speaks only one language. The only possibility is D. Complete the row with zeroes. From statement 4 we look for the three people who speak Portuguese. They cannot be C and E, since their common language was Italian. Therefore, two of the Portuguese speakers must be A and B. From statement 6 we need a person who speaks only two languages. It can only be E, so we write a zero for E in Portuguese. The third person who speaks Portuguese must be C, so we mark an X in the corresponding cell. We look now for the person who speaks three languages, and it can only be A. Fill in the row with zeroes. So, the person who speaks five languages is B. The table is now complete.

MISTER DIGIT FACE

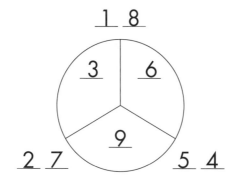

The 9 must be inside the circle, because no product can be 9_ or _9. The 1, 2, and 5 must be outside the circle. From here on you can find the solution. (Other answers can be made by flipping or rotating the circle.)

DIGIT TREE

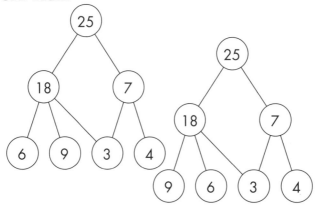

FIGURES TO CUT IN TWO

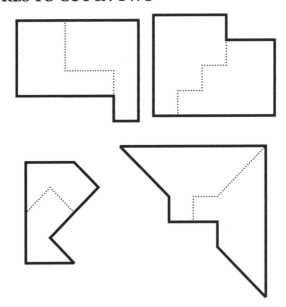

SEGMENTS

4	7	2	9	1	8	3	6	5

The numbers 4 and 5 must be at both ends because the sum of the nine digits is 45. Then we place 3 and 6, then 2 and 7, and finally 1, 8, and 9. (The order of the numbers can be reversed.)

MULTIPLE TOWERS

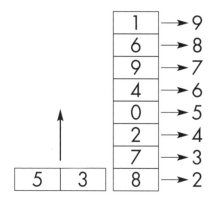

EARTHLINGS

Uruguay came in first, Spain second, Zaire third. The second earthling has one answer in common with the first one and one in common with the third one. In which category is the second earthling, then? He cannot always be telling the truth, because he has something in common with a liar, and he cannot always be lying because he has something in common with the honest one. If his first answer were true, then the third one would also be true, and they would be the same as the first and third answers from the honest man. There is no match, however, so this is not the case.

Therefore, the first answer from the man that alternately lies and tells the truth must be a lie. The second is true and the third a lie, so the third man is the honest one, and thus his answers are the results of the soccer championship.

THE ANT AND THE CLOCK

The ant walked 54 minutes. From the first meeting to the second, the minute hand traveled 45 minutes and the ant a distance in minute marks of 105 minutes (45 + a complete 60-minute lap). The illustration below shows the path followed by the ant. The speed ratio is 45/105 = 3/7. From the start to the first meeting, the minute hand traveled a distance X and the ant (30 – X). Using the speed ratio, this would be X/(30 – X) = 3/7. X = 9 minutes. If we add these to the 45 minutes that it took the ant to get to the second meeting, we come to 54 minutes for the ant's trip.

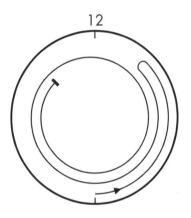

HIDDEN WORD—I
VISE

HIDDEN WORD—II
SOB

HIDDEN WORD—III
PITHY

SECRET NUMBER—I
3719

SECRET NUMBER—II
9381

SECRET NUMBER—III
2754

SECRET NUMBER—IV
2739

SECRET NUMBER—V
8327

CLASSIC BRAIN TWISTERS

DOMINOES — TABLE I

1	5	5	3	0	6	0	6
5	4	4	2	4	4	6	2
2	6	0	1	1	2	5	1
4	3	5	5	3	2	6	0
0	3	0	3	3	3	1	0
5	2	6	2	3	6	0	1
4	5	6	4	1	4	2	1

DOMINOES — TABLE II

3	1	2	2	6	1	3	4
5	5	3	4	0	5	3	2
2	6	5	1	1	2	0	0
1	1	0	6	0	3	3	0
0	6	4	3	6	5	4	5
3	2	5	4	0	1	6	2
5	4	6	4	2	4	6	1

DOMINOES — TABLE III

1	0	2	2	3	6	5
1	6	6	4	3	6	5
2	3	5	0	1	4	6
0	4	3	0	2	4	0
3	6	5	4	5	4	1
0	0	5	1	3	1	2
3	6	2	2	5	3	2
1	1	4	0	4	6	5

DOMINOES — TABLE IV

5	4	2	3	6	3	4
4	6	5	5	0	6	3
4	6	2	3	4	1	2
6	0	6	3	0	4	1
0	6	0	2	3	4	2
5	5	6	1	4	5	3
5	1	3	2	2	1	1
1	5	2	0	1	0	0

DOMINOES — TABLE V

4	0	0	1	1	1	0
5	2	3	5	6	5	6
3	5	4	4	3	4	2
2	0	0	5	6	5	3
2	2	1	5	6	0	1
2	4	4	3	2	6	4
5	6	0	3	2	3	6
1	1	3	6	4	1	0

DOMINOES — TABLE VI

4	5	1	6	0	5	1
2	5	3	5	3	6	5
6	2	0	4	2	2	6
6	6	2	0	5	3	3
3	1	1	2	3	6	4
4	0	3	1	0	0	4
4	1	2	1	4	5	3
5	1	2	0	0	4	6

HOUND—I

20	13	12	11	⑩
19	14	⑤	6	9
18	⑮	4	7	8
17	16	3	2	1

HOUND—II

25	26	27	㉘	29	30	31
24	15	⑭	㉟	34	33	32
23	16	13	12	11	8	⑦
22	17	18	1	10	9	6
㉑	20	19	2	3	4	5

HOUND—III

2	1	9	10	11
3	8	16	15	12
4	7	17	14	13
5	6	18	19	20
25	24	23	22	21

HOUND—IV

25	16	15	12	11
24	17	14	13	10
23	22	21	20	9
2	3	18	19	8
1	4	5	6	7

HOUND—V

There are two possible solutions.

(13)	12	(11)	8	(7)
14	15	10	9	6
(17)	16	(3)	4	(5)
18	1	(2)	25	24
(19)	20	21	22	(23)

(17)	16	(3)	4	(5)
18	15	(2)	1	6
(19)	14	(13)	12	(7)
20	(23)	24	(11)	8
21	22	25	10	9

POKER—I

J	10	J	K	A
8	8	8	A	8
Q	10	A	Q	Q
K	10	K	10	K
A	9	9	9	9

POKER—II

9	J	10	Q	K
J	J	Q	Q	Q
A	A	A	A	K
8	J	10	8	K
10	9	10	8	K

POKER—III

K	J	K	K	K
9	J	8	Q	10
9	8	J	Q	10
A	J	9	Q	10
A	8	8	A	10

POKER—IV

10	Q	K	J	A
8	8	K	8	8
J	10	K	Q	A
Q	J	K	10	A
9	9	9	9	A

POKER—V

9	A	9	A	A
8	Q	K	K	10
8	Q	K	J	J
8	A	9	J	10
8	Q	9	J	10

POKER—VI

10	Q	Q	Q	10
9	K	J	Q	10
A	K	A	A	A
8	K	J	8	10
J	K	J	8	9

BRAIN BAFFLERS
ANSWERS

1.   A = Adam; B = Joseph; C = Richard; D = Justin. The theme is boys' names.

2.   The numbers correspond to the alphabetical positions of the letters I, V, X, L, D and M; that is, the letters which are used in Roman numerals written in ascending order of value. The missing letter is "C", which in this sequence corresponds to 3.

3.   The semicircle and the tetrahedron are the next two shapes in the series.

   The six shapes are a cube, prism, circle, hexagon, cylinder, and rectangle. The number of letters in the name increases by one each time, from four to nine. Of the four shapes from which the seventh and eighth can be chosen, namely a square, tetrahedron, semicircle, and pyramid, only the semicircle and tetrahedron have 10 and 11 letters, respectively.

4.   Prime numbers of more than one digit end with 1, 3, 7, or 9, as do numbers that are three times prime numbers of more than one digit. Neither the third nor sixth digit of the required ten-digit number can be 7, and 9 cannot appear anywhere in the number. Knowing these facts helps narrow down the possibilities. The required number is 2,412,134,003.

5.   One solution is shown in the diagram.

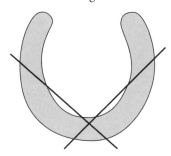

The second solution is to cut the horseshoe into three pieces with one cut, and then put them on top of one another for the next cut. The third solution is to cut the horseshoe in half along the plane of the page, and leaving these pieces on top of one another, cut each of these two pieces into three pieces.

6.   A = eyes; B = mouth; C = foot; D = spine. The theme is parts of the body.

7.   D = 100. Each letter equals the number in whose name it first appears. Thus tWo, foUr, fiVe and so on. D first occurs in one hunDreD.

8.   Our answer is "United States."

9.

D			
I	F		
S	E	A	
C	E	N	T

10.   Replace each letter in a country's name by the position of the letter in the alphabet. For example, Italy becomes 9 20 1 12 25. Goals scored is then the smallest difference between any pair of numbers, so Italy scores 12 – 9 = 3 goals.

The result of the final tie was therefore: Poland 1 Portugal 1.

11.   The last-numbered page in the book is number 141, and the missing leaf contains pages 5 and 6. Note that the seemingly alternative solution of the last-numbered page being 142 and the missing leaf being pages 76 and 77 does not work. This is because page 76 would be on the left and page 77 on the right, and therefore on different leaves.

12.   Across: 2. Parishioners, 3. Point, 4. Past due, 5. An aisle, 6. The Morse code, 7. Twelve + One, 8. Arguments. Down: 1. The nudist colony.

13.   A = Top Gun; B = Terms of Endearment; C = Born on the Fourth of July (the "y" is the fourth letter of "July"); D = Men in Black. The theme is films.

14.   29 days in February in a leap year
12 signs of the zodiac
7 wonders of the ancient world
54 cards in a deck (with the jokers)
32 degrees Fahrenheit, at which water freezes
18 holes on a golf course
4 quarts in a gallon
14 pounds in a stone

15.   2,025 or 3,025, as $(30 + 25)^2 - (20 + 25)^2 = 3,025 - 2,025 = 1,000$

16.

NAME	Mr. Gray	Mr. Brown	Mr. Green	Mr. Black	Mr. White
HOUSE	Blue	Maroon	Mauve	Yellow	Red
TOWN	Wagga Wagga	Woy Woy	Bong Bong	Peka Peka	Aka Aka
TEAM	Waratahs	Brumbies	Sharks	Hurricanes	Crusaders
PET	Kangaroo	Koala	Kookaburra	Kiwi	Kea

17.   A = buttercup; B = rose (homophone of rows); C = ivy (the clue is in roman numerals); D = hyacinth (high "a," "c" in "th"). The theme is plants.

18.   True. A tube designed to hold four tennis balls will be half full with two tennis balls and still half full with three tennis balls. This is because the volume of three tennis balls of unit radius is $3 \times 4/3\pi = 4\pi$ cubic units, which is half the volume of a cylinder of unit radius and eight units (four tennis balls) high.

19.   The two lists of words, with the reinserted letters shown uppercase, were as follows: **A**do, e**Bb**, **C**o**DE**, si**Ft**, **G**el, **H**e**I**r, **J**o**K**e, **L**u**M**i-

NOus, **P**ig, **QuaRtS**, **TU**g, li**V**e, **WaXY**, **Z**est; and do**Z**e, bo**Y**, si**X**, t**W**el**V**e, r**UT**, **SoRe**, **QuiP**, **ON**us, **MiLK**, **JI**g, **HuG**, **FatE**, gli**De**, **CaB**, e**A**st.

Minor variations are possible. For example, in the first set of words, "**CoDE**s, **F**it" could replace "**CoDE**, si**Ft**."

20.   Hawaii is the southernmost state and Alaska the northernmost and westernmost state. Less obviously, Alaska is also the easternmost state of the U.S.A. This is on account of the Aleutian Islands, which extend from the southwest corner of Alaska's mainland across the line of longitude 180° E/W.

21.   In addition to the information given directly in the question, note that if there is someone who last dined in restaurant A who will be dining next in restaurant B, then the person who last dined in restaurant B cannot be dining next in restaurant A. Working through the information given, the result below then follows:

NAME	CITY	LAST DINNER	NEXT DINNER
Ann	Auckland	Wholemeal Cafe	Farewell Spit Cafe
Ben	Dunedin	Collingwood Tavern	The Old School Cafe
Cathy	Christchurch	Milliways Restaurant	Wholemeal Cafe
David	Wellington	The Old School Cafe	Milliways Restaurant
Emma	Hamilton	Farewell Spit Cafe	Collingwood Tavern

22.   A = Bronx; B = Broadway; C = Central Park; D = Times Square. The theme is New York City.

23.   Across: 1. Postponed, 3. Other, 4. Astronomer, 5. HMS Pinafore, 6. Endearments, 7. A shoplifter, 8. The eyes. Down: 2. The countryside.

24.   One solution is for the digits 0, 1, 2, 3, 4 and 5 to appear on cube one and the digits 0, 1, 2, 6, 7 and 8 to appear on cube two. For dates that include the number 9, simply turn the 6 upside down.

25. Each number is put in a column according to the number of letters it has when it is written as a word. The first column contains all the numbers with three letters, the second column has all the numbers with four letters, and so on.

    A. 11 and 12 each have six letters when written as words, and so would appear in the fourth column.

    B. The final entry in the third column would be 60.

26. A = The Fifth Element; B = What Lies Beneath; C = Ghostbusters; D = Braveheart. The theme is films.

27. The paragraph is unusual because, unlike this answer, it does not contain the letter "e."

28.

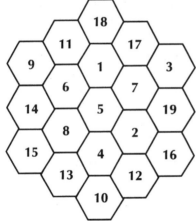

29. One, one, nine, three, and nine.

30. Yes, one, nine, three, nine, three, and nine.

31.   A = pony; B = dingo; C = sheep; D = lioness.
The theme is animals.

32.   Mozambique.

33.

N	N	F	X	I	S
E	E	I	O	W	T
I	V	V	N	U	H
G	E	E	E	E	R
H	S	Z	T	L	E
T	W	E	L	V	E

34.   It is not possible to end up with just one peg on the board if the central hole starts off empty. To show this, label the holes as shown:

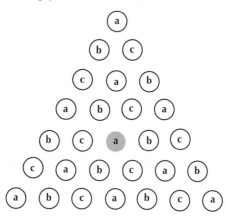

Initially there are nine pegs of each letter. After any move, the number of pegs in two of a, b, and c will be reduced by one, and the number of pegs in the holes of the remaining letter will be increased by one. Thus, at any stage, the number of pegs assigned to each letter will be either all odd or all even. Hence it is impossible to be left with only one peg on the board, for this would require an odd number (namely one) of pegs in holes of one particular letter and an even number (namely zero) of pegs in the holes of the two other letters.

35.   A = miner; B = gigolo; C = coroner; D = midwife. The theme is jobs.

36.   Yes, but only in the sense that the letters in each word are in alphabetical order.

37.   The seven solutions are: 0/0, 1/1, 8/512, 17/4,913, 18/5,832, 26/17,576, and 27/19,683. The four solutions where XSUM is a cube are: 0, 1, 8 and 27.

Note that XSUM = 64 = 4^3 cannot be a solution as X would then need to be at least an eight-digit number, yet 64^3 is only a six-digit number.

38.   The position for the cut of the block is shown in the diagram.
The side of the cut square is $\sqrt{9^2 + 9^2}$ inches = $\sqrt{(12^2 + 3^2 + 3^2)}$ inches, which is approximately 12.7 inches.

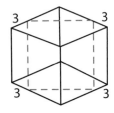

39.   Two unrelated women each married the other's son from a previous marriage. Each couple then had a daughter.

40.   1. Egypt   5. Vietnam
            2. Qatar   6. Senegal
            3. Brazil   7. Algeria
            4. Rwanda   8. Estonia

41.   Starting with the empty circle on the right and reading counter-clockwise, enter the letters "u," "n," and "d" so that "underground" can be spelled out. The less common word "undergrounder" is also formed from this circle.

42.   Luckily for Jimmy, yes!

43.

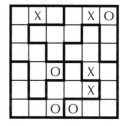

44.   The equation **TIM × SOLE = AMOUNT** is sufficient, with a computer search, to solve this puzzle. However, the extra information provided enables the puzzle to be solved as follows:

Because **LEAST** and **MOST** both end in **ST,** and either **LEAST − MOST = ALL** or **MOST − LEAST = ALL**, then **L** = 0.

Substituting **L** = 0 in **LEAST − MOST = ALL** and **MOST − LEAST = ALL**, then either **EA − MO = A** or **MO − EA = A.**

As **L** = 0, then **O** ≠ 0 so **EA − MO ≠ A** and **MO − EA = A.** From this, **MO = EA + A, M = E + 1,** and **O** is even. As **L** = 0, **O** = 2, 4, 6, or 8 and **A** = 6, 7, 8, or 9.

As **TIM × SOLE = AMOUNT**, then **M × E** is a number that ends with **T.** As we also know that **M = E + 1**, then **T** = 2 or 6. (Note that **T** ≠ 0 because **L** = 0.)

If **T** = 6, then **S** = 1 since **TIM** × **SOLE** is a six-digit number and **E** = 2 or 7.

If **T** = 6 and **E** = 2, then **M** = 3, **S** = 1 (see above), and **O** = 4 or 8. **O** ≠ 8, since **TIM** × **SOLE** is a six-digit number, and if **O** = 4, **A** = 7 and there is no solution, so this combination is eliminated.

If **T** = 6 and **E** = 7, then **M** = 8. However, then **A** = 9 and **O** = 8, which is impossible because **M** = 8. This combination is therefore also eliminated, and **T** = 2 because **T** ≠ 6.

Given that **T** = 2, then **E** = 3, 6, or 8 with corresponding values for **M** of 4, 7, and 9. Also, as **T** = 2, then **O** ≠ 2, so **O** = 4, 6, or 8 and **A** = 7, 8, or 9.

If **E** = 3 and **M** = 4, then **S** = 1 as **TIM** × **SOLE** is a six-digit number. But **T** = 2 and **S** = 1 implies **A** is less than 6, and **A** = 7, 8, or 9, so this combination is eliminated.

If **E** = 8 and **M** = 9, then **A** = 7 and **O** = 4. As **TIM** × **SOLE** is a six-digit number, **S** = 1 or 3, but then there is no solution, so this combination is eliminated.

Therefore **L** = 0, **T** = 2, **E** = 6, **M** = 7, **O** = 8, **A** = 9 and **S** = 3, from which **I** = 5, **U** = 1, and **N** = 4, giving 257 × 3,806 = 978,142.

45. A = clarinet; B = pianoforte; C = zither; D = double bass. The theme is musical instruments.

46.

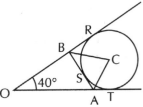

Angle O = 40°, so angles OAB + OBA = 180°− 40°= 140°
Angle TAS = 180°− angle OAB

Angle RBS = 180°− angle OBA
So angles TAS + RBS = 360°− 140°= 220°.
Since CA and CB bisect angles TAS and RBS, respectively, angles
    CAS + CBS = 110°.
Thus, angle ACB = 180°− 110°= 70°.
This angle is independent of the position of the tangent ASB.

47. $73 = \left(\sqrt{\sqrt{\sqrt{4}}}\right)^{4!} + \dfrac{4}{.\dot{4}}$ and $89 = \left(4! / \sqrt{.\dot{4}} - .4\right)/.4$
A dot over a decimal indicates that it is a repeating decimal.

48.   Across: 1. Cauldron, 3. Sort, 4. Stifle, 5. Meg Ryan, 6. Envelope, 8. Backwater (O to H is H_2O backwards). Down: 2. Desperation, 7. Edam.

49.   A = Monica; B = Andrea; C = Stephanie; D = Ingrid. The theme is girls' names.

50.   Suppose the army has advanced x miles before the commanding general receives the dispatch. The dispatch rider will then have ridden x + 4 miles.

The dispatch rider now rides (x + 4) − 4 = x miles back to where the army commenced its advance. The rider will arrive at this point at the same time as the rear of the army does and when the front of the army completes its 4 miles advance. Thus, the rider travels 2x + 4 miles while the army travels 4 miles.

Assuming constant speeds throughout, the ratio of the dispatch rider's speed to the army's speed will also be constant. Thus:

$$\frac{x + 4}{x} = \frac{2x + 4}{4}$$

from which $4x + 16 = 2x^2 + 4x$ and $x = \sqrt{8}$.

The dispatch rider travels 4 + 2x miles = 9.66 miles.

51.   Strychnine.

52.   Alan is from New Ze**al**and, Rita is from B**rita**in, Eric is from Am**eric**a, and Don is from In**don**esia.

53.   **THIS** = 5,693, **THAT** = 5,625, **IT** is 95, and **THIS** × **THAT** × **IT** = 3,042,196,875.

54.   N, being the last letter in the word "seven." The sequence is the last letters of the words one, two, three, etc.

55.   Let the dimensions of the hole be x by y inches, then: $1.25(2x + 2y) = xy$, from which $xy - 2.5x - 2.5y = 0$. This may be expressed as $(x - 2.5)(y - 2.5) = 6.25$.

The only integral solutions to this equation are $x = y = 5$, and $x = 15$ and $y = 3$ (or vice versa). Because the hole is wider than it is high, we require the latter solution, so the width of the hole for the letters is 15 inches.

56.   60,481,729, which is $(6,048 + 1,729)^2 = 7,777^2$.

57.   If Jill had said that the number was neither a perfect square nor perfect cube, then Jack would not have had enough information for an answer. Therefore, Jill must have said that the number was a square or a cube or both. The table below shows the possibilities:

Range	Squares	Cubes	Both
13–499	16, 25, 36, 49, 64, 81,	27, 64	64
	100, 121, 144, 169, 196,	125	
	225, 256, 289, 324, 361,	216	
	400, 441, 484	343	
500–1,300	529, 576, 625, 676, 729,	512	729
	784, 841, 900, 961, 1,024,	729	
	1,089, 1,156, 1,225, 1,296	1,000	

Jill could not have said that the number was a perfect square and a perfect cube; otherwise, Jack could have guessed the number after three questions.

If Jill had said that the number was a perfect square but not a perfect cube, then the fourth question would not have been sufficient to identify the number.

If Jill had said that the number was a perfect cube but not a perfect square, then the fourth question would have been sufficient to identify the number (512 or 1,000) only if Jill had said that the number was not below 500.

Jill therefore answered that the number was not below 500, was not a perfect square, but was a perfect cube. This tells us that the number is below 500, is a perfect square, and is a perfect cube. Therefore, Jill's number is 64.

58.   The favorite puzzle books were:

Alan	*Probability Paradoxes*	Emma	*Logic Puzzles*
Ben	*Brain Bafflers*	Fiona	*Mazes*
Claire	*Crosswords*	Gail	*Cryptograms*
Dave	*Number Games*	Henry	*Word Search*

59.   The first school had 495 pupils, of whom 286 were boys; the two schools combined had 1,495 pupils, of whom 415 were boys.

60.   A = scrambled eggs; B = banana split; C = cutlet; D = antipasto. The theme is food.

61.   Time flies? You cannot—they go too quickly. (If the meaning is still not apparent, "time" is used as a verb and "flies" as a noun.)

62.

WHITE	BLACK
1. P—KB3	N—KB3
2. P—K4	N x P
3. Q—K2	N—N6
4. Q x P ch	Q x Q ch
5. K—B2	N x R mate

The diagram shows the mate.

63.

WHITE	BLACK
1. P—KB3	N—QR3
2. P—QR4	N—N5
3. P—Q4	P—QB3
4. R—R3	Q—R4
5. R—Q3	N x R mate

The diagram shows the mate.

64. The answers to the clues are shown below. In each case, the first word is the one that is to be entered into the diagram:

ACROSS

7. palest/petals
8. secure/rescue
9. bizarre/brazier
11. alter/later

12. cater/trace
14. reliant/latrine
15. dieting/ignited
17. speak/peaks

20. scalp/claps
21. deposit/topside
23. shears/rashes
24. asleep/elapse

DOWN

1. manila/animal
2. sedate/seated
3. star/arts
4. detail/dilate
5. suitcase/sauciest

6. learnt/rental
10. enraged/angered
13. teenager/generate
15. disuse/issued

16. impart/armpit
18. poodle/looped
19. abides/biased
22. edam/mead

65.

A 4	a 2	b 9	B 4	c 1	Cd 2	0	D 9	e 9	f 2
Eg 7	5	F 2	h 9	G 5	6	4	Hi 7	7	4
I 8	8	j 1	J 9	K 1	k 1	0	5	l 1	
3	m 1	L 4	0	n 3	Mo 9	0	N 2	p 9	4
Oq 1	2	6	P 2	9	1	Q 9	r 3	R 8	4
S 3	3	0	T 3	9	U 2	1	V 6	4	4

66.   D scored no goals against A, and at most one goal against B.

D scored two goals in total, but did not win a game, so D's score against C was 1:1.

D drew against C and so lost to B, so D's score against B was 1:2.

All of B's goals, for and against, were in its match against D, so B's games with A and C were both 0:0.

By subtraction, A's scores against both C and D were 2:0.
The results are summarized below:

A vs B	0:0
A vs C	2:0
A vs D	2:0
B vs C	0:0
B vs D	2:1
C vs D	1:1

67. The number of possible arrangements is 42. To prove this, note that the positions of the 1 and the 9 are fixed. Now suppose that the 2 is placed below the 1. Then if the 3 is placed below the 2, five arrangements are possible. As an alternative, if the 3 is placed to the right of the 1, then there are five arrangements with the 4 under the 2, five with the 5 under the 2, four with the 6 under the 2, and two with the 7 under the 2. This gives a total of 21 arrangements. But by symmetry we would have another 21 if we had started by placing the 2 to the right of the 1, which gives a grand total of 42. (Notice that the digit in the center must be the 4, 5, or 6.)

68. The area of triangle ABC is $(25\sqrt{3} + 36)$ inches^2. To show this, consider any two of the triangles making up the equilateral triangle, say ABP and ACP (shown as ACP'). Place the two triangles together, AB on AC, to obtain the figure shown:

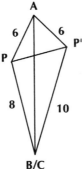

Angles PAB and CAP' total 60°, so PAP' is equilateral. Hence the quadrilateral APBP' can be regarded as an equilateral triangle with 6-inch sides on top of a right-angled triangle with sides 6, 8, and 10 inches. The overall area of the quadrilateral is therefore $(9\sqrt{3} + 24)$ inches^2.

By taking ABP and BCP, and ACP and BCP, other quadrilaterals can be constructed in a similar manner. Their areas are $(16\sqrt{3} + 24)$ inches^2 and $(25\sqrt{3} + 24)$ inches^2 respectively.

The total area of the three quadrilaterals so constructed is $(50\sqrt{3} + 72)$ inches^2. Because this counts each triangle within the original triangle twice, the area of triangle ABC is therefore $(25\sqrt{3} + 36)$ inches^2.

69. 24 hours in a day
5 vowels in the English alphabet
8 legs on a spider
1,000 words that a picture is worth
13 stripes on the American flag
14 lines in a sonnet
90 degrees in a right angle
9 lives of a cat

70.

3	71	5	23
53	11	37	1
17	13	41	31
29	7	19	47

71.

Let V = [log (1 + 1/1) + log (1 + 1/2) + log (1 + 1/3) + ... +
    log (1 + 1/9)] × 100%
Then V = [log (2/1) + log (3/2) + log (4/3) + ... + log (10/9)]
    × 100%
    = [log (2/1 × 3/2 × 4/3 × ... × 10/9)] × 100%
    = [log (10)] × 100%
    = 100%

72. The first drop should be from floor 14, and the maximum number of drops can be limited to no more than 14.

Suppose the first drop is from floor n. If the crystal breaks, then there is no alternative to dropping the second crystal from floor 1, then floor 2, and so on, up to floor (n – 1) at most. This would ensure that no more than n drops would be required.

Now suppose the crystal does not break on its drop from floor n. The second drop is then from floor (2n – 1), and if the crystal breaks here we start dropping the second crystal from floor n + 1, up to floor (2n – 2) at most. Again this ensures no more than n drops in total.

If the first crystal does not break, we continue advancing up the building by one less floor each time; i.e., by (n – 2), then (n – 3), and so on till we get to the top. We therefore need to find the smallest value of n such that n + (n –1) + (n – 2) + ... + 1 ≥ 105. (Remember, we already know that a crystal dropped from the 106th floor will shatter.)

The sum on the left-hand side simply gives the triangular number T_n = n(n + 1)/2, and if T_n ≥ 105, we then have n(n + 1) ≥ 210. The smallest value of n to satisfy this equation is 14.

73.   119 = ΣΣΣΣΣ√4 / ΣΣΣΣ√4 + Σ√4 = 26,796 / 231 + 3
268 = Σ(4!) – √ √4 ^{Σ4} = 300 – 32
336 = ΣΣ√4 × ΣΣ4 + ΣΣ√4 = 6 × 55 + 6

All integers from 1 to 336 can be made with three fours and the symbols given.

74. The fourth clue type is homophones.

S	P	O	I	L	T		S	P	I	T	E	F	U	L
L		N		I			O		R		A			E
P	A	W	S		D	E	C	O	R	A	T	I	O	N
C		T	I	E	R		R		C		L			I
S	A	R	I		O		E	X	E	C	U	T	E	
R		T		A	D	D	S		R			R		N
A	D	J	U	D	G	E		T	E	M	P	E	S	T
T			T		E				E		L			
O	F	F	E	N	D	S		C	I	T	A	D	E	L
D		A			E	X	I	T		S		N		
D	E	C	L	A	R	E		V		T	A	L	E	
B		U		N		S		I	D	L	E		A	
A	L	L	E	G	I	A	N	C	E		R	A	R	E
L		T		E		W		E		E		G		
L	O	Y	A	L	I	S	T		R	E	D	E	E	M

75. Apart from using the information given directly, clues can be combined for extra information. For example, clues one and three can be combined to deduce that Angela is not from Staten Island. Working through, the result below then follows.

MANAGER	ACCOUNT	DISTRICT	CHILDREN
Angela	Aviation	Bronx	4
Brian	Marine	Staten Island	3
Chloe	Liability	New Jersey	5
Dick	Fire	Queens	1
Enid	Automotive	Brooklyn	0
Fred	Property	Manhattan	2

76. Let the train be t minutes early. The wife (driving at 36 mph) saved 5 minutes each way, so the man walked for t – 5 minutes. Because this saved 5 minutes' driving, he walked at 5/(t – 5) of her speed. If she had driven at 46 mph, she would have saved 4 minutes each way, so similar reasoning leads to the following equation:

$$\frac{5}{t-5} \times 36 = \frac{4}{t-4} \times 46$$

whence t = 50 minutes.

77. Q is 67,980, and 54,321 × 67,980 = 3,692,741,580.

78.

Aa 7	0	Bb 3	c 1	5
C 8	d 2	1	D 9	e 9
E 4	5	Ff 8	6	4
G 3	2	0	H 7	6

79. A = goldfinch; B = eagle; C = partridge; D = nightingale. The theme is birds.

80. 3,015,986,724 = $54,918^2$ and 6,714,983,025 = $81,945^2$.

81. A. The tire wear after 1,000 miles will be: 1/18 + 1/18 + 1/22 + 1/22 = 20/99 of a tire. Five tires will therefore last 99/20 × 5 × 1,000 miles = 24,750 miles.

B. Four changes are needed, as shown below:

Miles	Front left	Front right	Rear left	Rear right	Spare
0–6,750	A	B	C	D	E
6,750–11,000	A	E	C	D	B
11,000–13,750	A	E	C	B	D
13,750–18,000	A	E	D	B	C
18,000–24,750	C	E	D	B	A

82.

The diagram shows the *ends* of the matches. There are six squares of unit size, and two squares measuring 2 × 2.

83.   The way for Lynsey to win is to play the dashed line shown below. Any other move would allow Heather the opportunity to win.

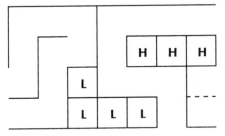

After claiming the two boxes in the bottom right-hand corner, Heather's best move is to open up the nine boxes at the top right and center and hope that Lynsey will take them. Lynsey would be wrong to do so, however, for she can win by the strategy shown below of taking just seven boxes:

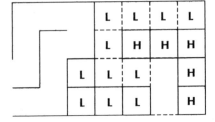

Lynsey's sacrifice of two boxes forces Heather to open up the group of ten boxes on the left-hand side for Lynsey. The final result would be as shown below, with Lynsey winning by 21 boxes to 7.

L	L	L	L	L	L	L
L	L	L	L	H	H	H
L	L	L	L	L	H	H
L	L	L	L	L	H	H

Note that if Lynsey had originally offered Heather the chance of completing the two boxes in the bottom right-hand corner with a vertical line instead of the one shown, Heather could have taken control of the game simply by adding another vertical line to the bottom right-hand corner.

84. 95,759.

85. Label Samos Farm as shown below:

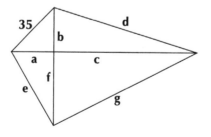

Thus $a^2 + b^2 = 35^2$, $b^2 + c^2 = d^2$, $c^2 + f^2 = g^2$ and $a^2 + f^2 = e^2$, where $a, b, c, d, e, f,$ and g are all different, integral, and not equal to 35.

The unique integral solution to $a^2 + b^2 = 35^2$ is $21^2 + 28^2 = 35^2$. Other integral Pythagorean triangles with a side of 21 or 28 are:

$$21^2 + 20^2 = 29^2 \qquad 28^2 + 45^2 = 53^2$$
$$21^2 + 72^2 = 75^2 \qquad 28^2 + 96^2 = 100^2$$
$$21^2 + 220^2 = 221^2 \qquad 28^2 + 195^2 = 197^2$$

Assuming a is 21 and b is 28 (it does not matter which way around), f is 20, 72, or 220, and c is 45, 96, or 195. Knowing that $\sqrt{(f^2 + c^2)}$ is integral, the only possible values of f and c are 72 and 96. The area of the farm can now be calculated and is: $\frac{1}{2}(21 \times 28 + 21 \times 72 + 96 \times 28 + 96 \times 72) / 10 = (21 + 96) \times (28 + 72) / 20 = 585$ acres.

86. $1! + 4! + 5! = 145$.

87. As with many puzzles such as this, the flaw is in the given diagram. A more accurate diagram is shown here:

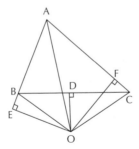

Proceeding as before:
AFO is congruent to AEO, so AE = AF and OE = OF.
BDO is congruent to CDO, so OB = OC.
OEB is congruent to OFC, so EB = FC.
Thus, AE + EB = AF + FC = AC $\neq$ AB, because AB = AE – EB.

88.   A = Orlando; B = Cincinnati; C = New Orleans; D = Washington, DC. The theme is American cities.

89.

90.   Starting with the lower right empty circle and reading counter-clockwise, enter the letters "i," "s," and "t" so that "strategist" can be spelled out.

91.   The sound of each letter in the top row is the same as a three-letter word that does not include the letter itself: sea, eye, eau (as in eau de Cologne), cue, and ewe.

92.   White wins as follows:

WHITE	BLACK
1. R – QR3	P – N6
2. R – R1	P x R (Q ch)
3. Q x Q mate	

93.

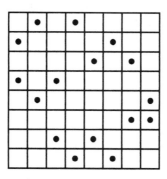

94.

C				
H	E			
E	A	R		
C	R	O	W	
K	N	E	E	L

95. Ask A, "Does B tell the truth more often than C?" If the answer is yes, then ask C the next two questions and if the answer is no, ask B. This question is designed to ensure that the second and third questions will not be directed at the man who lies at random.

Question two is: "Do the other two always give the same answer?" As the truthful answer is always "No," this question determines whether the man being asked is the one that is always truthful or the one that always lies.

Question three is: "Of the other two, does A tell the truth more often?" The answer will enable you to determine the status of the other two men.

96.

1 3	2 5	3 8	4 8	5 9	6 6
7 5	3	7	6	0	1
8 1	2	3	4	6	7
9 7	9	6	1	5	3
9	7	10 1	7	3	9

97. Begin by noting that the cake's area cannot be less than $(1 \times 10) + (2 \times 9) + (3 \times 8) + (4 \times 7) + (5 \times 6) = 110$ inches^2. By trial and error, the smallest cake that will meet the requirements will then be found to be 9 × 13 inches, which has an area of 117 inches^2. The cut cake is as shown:

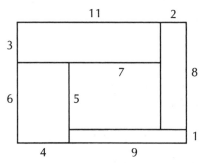

98. A = mandolin; B = oboe; C = triangle; D = cymbals (symbols). The theme is musical instruments.

99. The Statue of Liberty.

100.

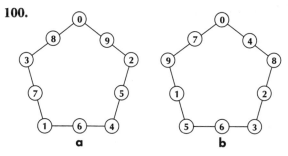

Other answers to b are possible.

101. One solution is to weigh 1 + 2 + 3 against 4 + 5 + 6, and 1 + 5 + 7 against 2 + 4 + 8, 1 + 4 against 2 + 5, and 3 + 6 against 7 + 8. From the results of these four weighings, it can be ascertained which, if any, are the lighter and heavier mince pies.

102. Our answer is "Booby prize."

103. Britney Spears is an anagram of Presbyterians.

104. David, of course. Read the question!

105. $153 = 1! + 2! + 3! + 4! + 5!$ and $153 = 1^3 + 5^3 + 3^3$. Also, $371 = 3^3 + 7^3 + 1^3$.

106.

Aa 1	b 2	7	c 3	d 3	6	e 3	f 2
B 1	0	g 2	4	C 3	h 5	6	8
7	D 2	4	8	8	3	2	0
E 6	5	6	1	F 1	1	2	7
G 9	i 8	0	j 1	Hk 8	4	l 6	4
2	I 1	1	7	6	4	9	8
J 6	9	6	2	K 4	1	4	1
L 1	1	3	8	9	8	9	6

107. A = Hyundai; B = BMW; C = Honda; D = Bentley. The theme is cars.

108. The statements can be rewritten as follows:
- Today is Thursday.
- Today is Tuesday.
- Today is Sunday.
- Today is Sunday, Monday, Tuesday, Wednesday, Thursday, or Friday.
- Today is Tuesday.
- Today is Wednesday, Thursday, Friday, or Saturday.
- Today is Monday.

The only day that is not mentioned more than once is Saturday, so today must be Saturday.

109.   (A) 1,357 × 2,468 = 3,349,076
(B) 8,531 × 7,642 = 65,193,902

110.   The easiest way to solve this puzzle is to note that the 5 × 5 checkerboard must have 13 squares of one color and 12 of the other. Now, if the cross-shaped piece is excluded, the remaining five pieces comprise 14 white and 11 black squares. Thus the cross-shaped piece must be used.

It is then not too difficult to find the following solution (piece 1 is not used):

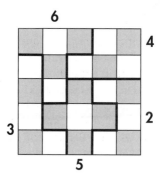

111.   Vivienne Westwood had 153 outfits exhibited. The "3" represents the number of letters appearing only once in her name (i.e., the "s," "t," and "d"); the "5" represents the number of letters appearing twice (the "v," "i," "n," "w," and "o"); and the "1" represents the number of letters appearing three times (the "e").

112.   The middle circle reads New Zealand, and the five six-letter words are "snooze," "secede," "casino," "meddle," and "Malawi."

282 CLASSIC BRAIN TWISTERS

113. Barbara Easton weighs 117 pounds, after losing three pounds.
Anne Frost weighs 113 pounds, after losing two pounds.
Debbie Green weighs 101 pounds, after losing four pounds.
Carol Hope weighs 111 pounds, after gaining one pound.

114. One solution is:

	3	5	
7	1	8	2
	4	6	

115. From the information given in the question, we know that the radius of the outer circle (the one on which A and B lie) is 3 times the radius of the inner, concentric circle through C and D. Thus, the circumference of the outer circle is 3 times the circumference of the inner circle, and so the arcs AB and CD are equal in length.

Since arc CD is more curved than arc AB, its ends will be closer together. Thus, the lines AC and BD are not parallel—they will meet down and to the left of the diagram.

116. The missing number is 244,769. This is calculated by adding the number to its left to the product of the two numbers above them. In this case, $6,949 + 1,081 \times 220$. An example from the grid is $220 = 31 + 21 \times 9$.

117. The common total is 21. A = 3, B = 4, and C = 5.

118. Suppose n clients were picked, with 10n names in the complete mailing list. The clients picked were numbers 1, 3, 6, 10, ... with the final one being number $n(n + 1)/2$. Since the final one was the last name in the index, it follows that $10n = n(n + 1)/2$, whence $20 = n + 1$. Thus, 19 clients were chosen out of a total mailing list of 190 clients.

ANSWERS
Brain Bafflers

119. Apart from its mirror image, the four-by-six solution below is unique.

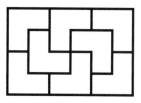

120. Remarkably, five queens are still sufficient.

121. $0.56, $1.20, $1.25, $1.50, $1.70, $2.00, and $2.50.

122.   Ring D goes over B, which goes over A, which goes over D. Thus, the rubber ring must be A, B, or D. Similarly, B goes over C, which goes over E, which goes over B. The common ring in each case is B, so it must be the rubber one.

123.   Labeling the engines, wagons, and different parts of the track as shown will make the solution given here (there is at least one other) easier to follow:

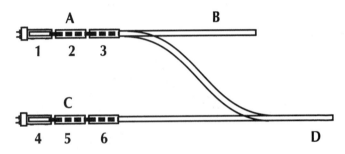

Move 123 to B and uncouple 3. Return 12 to A.

Move 456 to D and uncouple 5 and 6.

Move 12 toward D and couple with 5. Return 125 to A.

Move 125 to B, uncouple 5 and return 12 to A.

Move 12 toward D, leaving 2 in D, where it is picked up by 4 and taken to C.

1 picks up 5 and 3 from B and leaves 3 in D.

42 picks up 3 and returns to C.

Finally 15 picks up 6 from D and returns to A.

INDEX